Treasures
Old and New

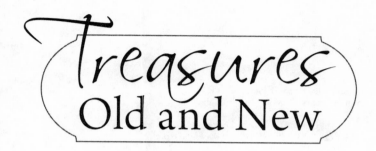

Treasures
Old and New

Traditional Prayers
for Today's Catholics

Philip Neri Powell, OP

Liguori
LIGUORI, MISSOURI

Imprimi Potest: Thomas D. Picton, C.Ss.R.
Provincial, Denver Province, The Redemptorists

Published by Liguori Publications, Liguori, Missouri
To order, call 800-325-9521 or visit www.liguori.org

Library of Congress Cataloging-in-Publication Data

Powell, Philip Neri.
  Treasures old and new : traditional prayers for today's Catholics / Philip Neri Powell.
—1st ed.
    p. cm.
  ISBN 978-0-7648-1840-0
  1. Catholic Church--Prayers and devotions. I. Title.
  BX2149.2.P69 2009
  242'.802--dc22

                                                          2009024015

Liguori Publications, a nonprofit corporation, is an apostolate of the Redemptorists. To learn more about the Redemptorists, visit Redemptorists.com.   •

Printed in the United States of America
13 12 11 10 09   5 4 3 2 1
First Edition

Contents

Foreword

All one has to do is browse the aisles of any major retail bookstore to draw the conclusion that there is a lively and deep thirst for spirituality in the midst of an increasingly unfriendly—even hostile—attitude toward traditional faith and religion. So many of the paths being offered by the spiritual gurus of the day will never satisfy that thirst in any sustainable way and certainly will never fully quench it. Often the unwitting thirsty sojourner discovers somewhere along the way that this God-given, God-centered, God-directed desire and longing has been subtly reoriented toward a dead-end trap of self-worship. It is important to remember that our Catholic tradition holds many beautiful and valuable treasures which have served for centuries to guide the spiritually thirsty, not to the narcissistic pond of self-reflection, but to the infinitely flowing river of living water.

Dominican Friar, Father Philip Neri Powell, OP, has retrieved such Catholic treasures in this book of litanies, novenas, and special prayers. This volume is a wonderful introduction for some and a re-introduction for others to a solidly Catholic way of entering into a prayer relationship with the One who created us, who sustains us, and who desires to spend eternity with us. Father Philip's unique contribution lies in his adaptations of traditional litanies and novenas for modern use (in the best sense of that term) and his creative authorship of several original litanies, novenas, and special prayers. His concise treatment of "A Theology of Prayer," an added bonus, is insightful and provides a basic catechesis for both the seasoned pray-er and the novice. All of what is contained in this wonderful little book flows beautifully out of the Dominican intellectual tradition and the richness of the Order's spirituality, as well as Father Philip's solid personal foundation in theology, philosophy, and English literature.

Those who are moved to pray with *Treasures Old and New* will be invited onto a tried and true path that will begin to quench their spiritual thirst as they approach our loving God with both mind and heart in a spirit of humility, gratitude, and praise.

FR. MARTIN J. GLEESON, OP
PRIOR PROVINCIAL
DOMINICAN FRIARS
PROVINCE OF ST. MARTIN DE PORRES
NEW ORLEANS, LOUISIANA

Preface

Worried that my studies in the philosophy of science and interpretation were taking me away from the more affective side of my spiritual life, I went looking for a devotional practice that would keep my prayer life grounded in both heart and head. It did not take long for me to discover that most traditional Catholic devotions were entirely too sentimental for my Dominican tastes. When I looked around for less sentimental texts, I found bad theology and worse spirituality.

I was once told by a revered Dominican friar, "We feel with our heads and think with our hearts. Prayer is study. Study is prayer." With this in mind, I decided to adapt some of the more traditional devotional prayers, toning down the sentiment and cleaning up the theology.

You might wonder why I think sentimentalism in prayer is troublesome. We are most like God in our intellectual faculties. This in no way diminishes the importance of the will. In fact, when our willed responses are rightly governed by reason and not simply indulged, we swiftly approach the horizons of holiness. But deeply embedded in the human person is a pestering gift: the desire to love; that is, an ingrained need to do and be the good for others. This is a passion for us, not just a sentiment. Loving rightly is our principal means of participating in the divine life.

One of the spiritual dangers of loving inordinately is the possibility that we will be overwhelmed by tumultuous emotion. To feel anger, impatience, dread, joy is not troublesome in itself. However, to allow these to overcome and rule what makes us most like God is very troublesome. Sentimentalism is a temptation to wallow in unchecked emotion, to indulge in mere feeling at the expense of right reason.

I must also point out the dangers of intellectualism. Inordinately privileging the intellect at the expense of the will (thinking the good but not doing it) quickly leads to quietism and apathy. Exercising our intellectual gifts in the service of truth in no way requires us to abandon our duty to work for justice. We cannot do just works, much less be just people, if we resolve to think just thoughts alone. Arguments, evidence, syllogisms, intellectual work are all well and good, even necessary, but it is when we love in the knowledge of God's wisdom that we drink most deeply of the divine.

Accordingly, I hope to accomplish two related goals with this book of adapted, edited, and original devotions. First, I want to provide contemporary Catholics with devotional texts that are both effectively rich and intellectually sound. Second, I want these texts to be not only devotional, but catechetical as well. By praying these texts, my hope is that you will not only give thanks and praise to God, but also grow in knowledge and understanding of the faith. In other words, I pray you will learn to think with your heart and feel with your head.

The devotions in this book are written for group prayer. The novenas contain meditations on the daily readings that invite individual reflection. This too can be done in small groups. In fact, the novenas can be used for small group study and prayer in a parish or school setting. Adapting these devotions to individual prayer is as easy as shifting pronouns from the plural to the singular. I have intentionally chosen texts for the readings that will challenge you to grow beyond easy sentiment and safe ideas. Our spiritual heritage as Catholics is too rich and varied to settle for tears without thought and ideas without affection. Wrestle with these texts as you would a temptation. But these are temptations you might let win.

Introduction

A Theology of Prayer

Praying as Christians does not come to us naturally. Crying out for help; wishing for something better; saying "thank you" under our breath—all of these seem to come to us naturally; that is, they all seem to arise out of some deeply held sense that there is something or someone "out there" to whom we ought to address our most intimate words, something or someone out there that we need to address, that we want to talk to and with.

But what we Christians might want to think of as a natural tendency to incline our deepest groans toward "something larger" is really a supernatural gift that makes us want to seek our perfection. Human prayer *per se* might be a natural inclination. Christian prayer is an entirely different sort of inclination altogether.

First, Christian prayer—a baptized person's internal and external conversation with God—is made possible by the life, death, and resurrection of our Lord, Jesus Christ. To be baptized is to be brought through and along with the Paschal Mystery that offers all rational creatures salvation in Christ. When a Christian prays, he prays as Christ prays; that is, he is Christ praying. Therefore, no Christian ever prays without the prompting of the Holy Spirit. We pray because the Holy Spirit nudges us and says, "Hey, this is a good time to pray, dontcha think?"

Second, to be brought through and along with the Paschal Mystery is to be made Christ for others. There is no other reason for us to be made Christs in this world except to be made Christs for others. If our creation *ex nihilo* was a gift (and it was!), and if your continuing existence is a gift (and it is!), and if our reconciliation to our Creator is a gift (and it is!), and if our eternal lives with him as his perfected creatures is his gift (and it will be!), then if we are to honor these gifts (which is really just one gift), we must be gifts ourselves to and for others.

Third, we are gifts—for one other. The only proper response to a gift is gratitude. Certainly, after receiving a gift, we respond with a "thank you." But in the life of a Christian, life itself is a gift. That you are here at all is a gift. Every blessing after this first blessing of life is gravy. Therefore, give thanks now for every blessing you will ever be given. In fact, make it a discipline to make your only prayer a prayer of thanksgiving for all the blessings you have received, are receiving, and will ever receive. A gift is not a gift until it is received as such. So, your prayer for others should be, "Lord, thank you for the blessings/gifts you have given, are giving, and will give to me, my family, and my neighbors." Remember: our Lord will not force a blessing/gift on you. Receive and give thanks.

Fourth, prayer is participation; that is to say, to pray is to play, to go along with, to share in and contribute toward. When you pray for yourself and especially for others, you are exercising your baptismal ministry as a royal priest. Think of praying as being submerged in water. Surrounded by God's life-giving grace, you live and move and work and play in his gifts. As a gift, you are at home among his gifts. Prayer then is our primary way of being with God, being in God, participating in his work and partaking of his divine nature. The supreme and insurmountable moment of prayer for the Christian is the Eucharist, that moment in our ecclesial life when Christ offers Christ to Christ through the priestly office of Christ for his Body, the Church!

Finally, because we are imperfect creatures on the road to perfection with the help of God's grace, we must come to accept the reality that the first person changed by prayer is the pray-er. God is not changed by prayer. There is no magic in prayer. Novenas, Masses, candles, processions—none of these change God. Our Lord is not some forest god who can be influenced with promises or bribed with sacrifices. The point of prayer, the whole purpose of prayer is to change the pray-er so that the pray-er may be better prepared to receive God's gifts in gratitude. Gratitude prepares the soul for humility; humility makes prayer come more easily. The more we rest and work and play in prayer, we more we come to resemble prayer itself—the Word spoken to the Word in thanksgiving.

Part One
The Novenas

Credo Novena

Early in the history of the Church, believers often found themselves confronted by any number of competing versions of the faith. Most of these were heretical deviations from the catholic faith of the apostles. Some were theological explanations of revelation that made extensive use of the Greek philosophical terms and concepts. So that the faithful might have a solid foundation upon which to build their lives in Christ, the bishops of the Church met in Nicaea in 325 AD. These bishop-theologians wrestled with the problem of how to incorporate the fundamental tenets of the Christian teaching into language that would exclude from the faith the prominent heresies of the day. The bishops of Nicaea produced the Nicene Creed. Meeting again in Constantinople in 381 AD, the bishops revised the Nicene Creed in order to further clarify basic Christian teaching. It was common among the early Church Fathers to use the creed as a kind of textbook for teaching those just entering the Church at Easter (i.e., "catechumens"). Today, we use this ancient creed in the celebration of the Eurcharist to reaffirm our faith. The commentary on the creed in this novena is taken from the work, "A Sermon to Catechumins on the Creed," written by St. Augustine.

Daily Opening Prayer

In you, O Lord, we place our trust.
>   *You who reign forever.*
With you, O Lord, we trust our lives.
In you, O Lord, we place our trust.

Almighty and living God, always and everywhere we seek the truth of your Word, to live and love as we ought. Knowing that we are always tempted by the wisdom of this world to abandon our faith in you and take after alien philosophies, your servants composed a creed that guides us to this day. Though we make no claims to absolute understanding, we confess a ravenous hunger for knowing more and better the teachings of Christ given to his Apostles. As we contemplate the truths of this creed, open our hearts and minds to all that you would teach us. Grant us peace without complacency, certainty without arrogance, and goodness in all humility. In Christ's name we pray. Amen.

Daily Hymn (for Each Day)

O Lord, our Sovereign,
*   how majestic is your name in all the earth!*

You have set your glory above the heavens.
*   Out of the mouths of babes and infants*
you have founded a bulwark because of your foes,
*   to silence the enemy and the avenger.*
When I look at your heavens, the work of your fingers,
*   the moon and the stars that you have established;*
what are human beings that you are mindful of them,
*   mortals that you care for them?*

Yet you have made them a little lower than God,
*   and crowned them with glory and honour.*
You have given them dominion over the works of your hands;
*   you have put all things under their feet,*
all sheep and oxen,
*   and also the beasts of the field,*
the birds of the air, and the fish of the sea,
*   whatever passes along the paths of the seas.*

O Lord, our Sovereign,
*   how majestic is your name in all the earth!*

PSALM 8

Alternate:

The Lord is my rock, my fortress, and my deliverer,
my God, my rock in whom I take refuge,
my shield, and the horn of my salvation, my stronghold.
call upon the Lord, who is worthy to be praised;
so I shall be saved from my enemies.

He brought me out into a broad place;
he delivered me, because he delighted in me.

With the loyal you show yourself loyal;
with the blameless you show yourself blameless;
with the pure you show yourself pure;
and with the crooked you show yourself perverse.

The Lord lives! Blessed be my rock,
and exalted be the God of my salvation,

For this I will extol you, O Lord, among the nations,
and sing praises to your name.
Great triumphs he gives to his king,
and shows steadfast love to his anointed,
to David and his descendants for ever.

PSALM 18:2–3, 19, 25–26, 46, 49–50

Daily Closing Prayer (for Each Day)

Lord God, we stand on you, the sure foundation revealed to us in your Son, Christ Jesus. We proclaim as true all that this creed contains and vow again to teach and preach only these truths. By baptism we entered your coming kingdom, dedicating ourselves to the apostolic faith. Grant us every grace, every talent, every virtue we need to hold fast to you. May this creed be a shining light on the way to you. In Christ's name, we pray. Amen.

DAY ONE

We believe in one God, the Father, the Almighty, of all that is, seen and unseen.

Daily Opening Prayer

God is Almighty, and yet, though Almighty, He cannot die, cannot be deceived, cannot lie; and, as the Apostle says, "cannot deny Himself."...To our Almighty Father, it is quite impossible to sin. He does whatsoever He will: that is Omnipotence. He does whatsoever He rightly will, whatsoever He justly will: but whatsoever is evil to do, He wills not....It was He Who made heaven and earth, the sea, and all that in them is, invisible and visible. Invisible such as are in heaven, thrones, dominions, principalities, powers, archangels, angels: all, if we shall live aright, our fellow-citizens. He made in heaven the things visible; the sun, the moon, the stars. With its terrestrial animals He adorned the earth, filled the air with things that fly, the land with them that walk and creep, the sea with them that swim: all He filled with their own proper creatures. He made also man after His own image and likeness, in the mind: for in that is the image of God. This is the reason why the mind cannot be comprehended even by itself, because in it is the image of God.

"A SERMON TO CATECHUMINS ON THE CREED," 2

Daily Hymn

Daily Closing Prayer

DAY TWO

We believe in one Lord, Jesus Christ, the only Son of God, eternally begotten of the Father, God from God, Light from Light, true God from true God; begotten, not made, of one Being with the Father. Through him all things were made.

Daily Opening Prayer

Man begets not an ox, sheep begets not dog, nor dog sheep. Whatever it be that begets, that which it is, it begets. Hold ye therefore boldly, firmly, faithfully, that the Begotten of God the Father is what Himself is, Almighty....He that is begotten mortal generates that which himself is; the Immortal generates what He is: corruptible begets corruptible, Incorruptible begets Incorruptible: the corruptible begets corruptibly, Incorruptible, Incorruptibly: yea, so begets what Itself is, that One begets One, and therefore Only....Here too, when you believe that He is the Only, believe Him Almighty: for it is not to be thought that God the Father does what He will, and God the Son does not what He will. One Will of Father and Son, because one Nature. For it is impossible for the will of the Son to be any whit parted from the Father's will. God and God; both one God: Almighty and Almighty; both One Almighty....The Son of God...was begotten perfect. And being begotten perfect, if He grows not, and remained not less, He is equal. For that you may know Almighty begotten of Almighty, hear Him Who is Truth. That which of Itself Truth says, is true. What says Truth? What says the Son, Who is Truth?

"A SERMON TO CATECHUMINS ON THE CREED," 3, 5

Daily Hymn

Daily Closing Prayer

DAY THREE

For us men and for our salvation he came down from heaven: by the power of the Holy Spirit he became incarnate from the Virgin Mary, and was made man.

Daily Opening Prayer

...this Only Son of God, the Father Almighty, let us see what He did for us, what He suffered for us....He, so great God, equal with the Father, born of the Holy Ghost and of the Virgin Mary, born lowly, that so that He might heal the proud. Man exalted himself and fell; God humbled Himself and raised him up. Christ's lowliness, what is it? God has stretched out a hand to man laid low. We fell, He descended: we lay low, He stooped. Let us lay hold and rise, that we fall not into punishment. So then His stooping to us is this, "Born of the Holy Ghost and of the Virgin Mary." His very Nativity too as man, it is lowly, and it is lofty. Whence lowly? That as man He was born of men. Whence lofty? That He was born of a virgin. A virgin conceived, a virgin bore, and after the birth was a virgin still.

"A SERMON TO CATECHUMINS ON THE CREED," 6

Daily Hymn

Daily Closing Prayer

DAY FOUR

For our sake he was crucified under Pontius Pilate; he suffered death and was buried. On the third day he rose again in accordance with the Scriptures; he ascended into heaven and is seated at the right hand of the Father.

Daily Opening Prayer

Of His cross what shall I speak, what say? This extremest kind of death He chose, that not any kind of death might make His Martyrs afraid. The doctrine He showed in His life as Man, the example of patience He demonstrated in His Cross. There, you have the work, that He was crucified; example of the work, the Cross; reward of the work, Resurrection. He showed us in the Cross what we ought to endure, He showed in the Resurrection what we have to hope. Just like a consummate task-master in the matches of the arena, He said, Do, and bear; do the work and receive the prize; strive in the match and you shall be crowned. What is the work? Obedience. What the prize? Resurrection without death. Why did I add, "without death?" Because Lazarus rose, and died: Christ rose again, "dies no more, death will no longer have dominion over Him."

"A SERMON TO CATECHUMINS ON THE CREED," 9

Daily Hymn

Daily Closing Prayer

DAY FIVE

He will come again in glory to judge the living and the dead, and his kingdom will have no end.

Daily Opening Prayer

The quick, who shall be alive and remain; the dead, who shall have gone before. It may also be understood thus: The living, the just; the dead, the unjust. For He judges both, rendering unto each his own. To the just He will say in the judgment, Come, you blessed of My Father, receive the kingdom prepared for you from the beginning of the world. For this prepare yourselves, for these things hope, for this live, and so live, for this believe, for this be baptized, that it may be said to you, Come ye blessed of My Father, receive the kingdom prepared for you from the foundation of the world. To them on the left hand, what? Go into everlasting fire prepared for the devil and his angels. Thus will they be judged by Christ, the quick and the dead. We have spoken of Christ's first nativity, which is without time; spoken of the other in the fullness of time, Christ's nativity of the Virgin; spoken of the passion of Christ; spoken of the coming of Christ to judgment. The whole is spoken, that was to be spoken of Christ, God's Only Son, our Lord....

"A SERMON TO CATECHUMINS ON THE CREED," 12

Daily Hymn

Daily Closing Prayer

DAY SIX

We believe in the Holy Spirit, the Lord, the giver of life, who proceeds from the Father and the Son. With the Father and the Son he is worshipped and glorified. He has spoken through the Prophets.

Daily Opening Prayer

This Trinity, one God, one nature, one substance, one power; highest equality, no division, no diversity, perpetual dearness of love. Would ye know the Holy Ghost, that He is God? Be baptized, and you will be His temple.... A temple is for God: thus also Solomon, king and prophet, was bidden to build a temple for God. If he had built a temple for the sun or moon or some star or some angel, would not God condemn him? Because therefore he built a temple for God he showed that he worshipped God. And of what did he build? Of wood and stone, because God deigned to make unto Himself by His servant an house on earth, where He might be asked, where He might be had in mind.... If then our bodies are the temple of the Holy Ghost, what manner of God is it that built a temple for the Holy Ghost? But it was God. For if our bodies be a temple of the Holy Ghost, the same built this temple for the Holy Ghost, that built our bodies. Listen to the Apostle saying, "God has tempered the body, giving unto that which lacked the greater honor;" when he was speaking of the different members that there should be no schisms in the body. God created our body. The grass, God created; our body Who created? How do we prove that the grass is God's creating? He that clothes, the same creates.... He, then, creates Who clothes.... If then it be God that builds our bodies, God that builds our members, and our bodies are the temple of the Holy Ghost, doubt not that the Holy Ghost is God. And do not add as it were a third God; because Father and Son and Holy Ghost is One God. So believe you.

"A SERMON TO CATECHUMINS ON THE CREED," 13

Daily Hymn

Daily Closing Prayer

DAY SEVEN
We believe in one, holy, catholic, and apostolic Church.

Daily Opening Prayer
God is pointed out, and His temple. "For the temple of God is holy," says the Apostle, "which (temple) are you." This same is the holy Church, the one Church, the true Church, the catholic Church, fighting against all heresies: fight, it can: be fought down, it cannot. As for heresies, they went all out of it, like as unprofitable

branches pruned from the vine: but the faith itself abides in roots of the Church, in its Vine, in its charity. "The gates of hell shall not prevail against it."

"A SERMON TO CATECHUMINS ON THE CREED," 14

Daily Hymn

Daily Closing Prayer

DAY EIGHT

We acknowledge one baptism for the forgiveness of sins.

Daily Opening Prayer

You have the Creed perfectly in you when you receive Baptism. Let none say, "I have done this or that sin: maybe that sin is not forgiven me." What have you done? How great a sin have you done? Name any heinous thing you have committed, heavy, horrible, which you shudder even to think of; anything have done: have you killed Christ? There is no deed any worse, because there is nothing better than Christ....When you have been baptized, hold fast to a good life in the commandments of God, that you may guard your Baptism even unto the end. I do not tell you that you will live here without sin; but they are venial. This life is not without venial sin. For the sake of all sins was Baptism provided; for the sake of minor sins, without which we cannot be, was prayer provided. What is the Prayer? "Forgive us our debts, as we also forgive our debtors." Once for all we have washing in Baptism, every day we have washing in prayer....In three ways then are sins remitted in the Church; by Baptism, by prayer, by the greater humility of penance...

"A SERMON TO CATECHUMINS ON THE CREED," 15, 16

Daily Hymn

Daily Closing Prayer

DAY NINE
We look for the resurrection of the dead, and the life of the world to come.

Daily Opening Prayer
We believe also "the resurrection of the flesh," which went before us in Christ, so that the body too may have hope of resurrecting as did its Head. The Head of the Church, Christ: the Church, the body of Christ. Our Head is risen, ascended into heaven: where the Head is there also are the members. In what way do we understand resurrection? So that none might think it like Lazarus's resurrection, that you may know it to be not so, the creed adds, "into life everlasting." God regenerate you! God preserve and keep you! God bring you safe unto Himself, Who is the Life Everlasting. Amen.

"A SERMON TO CATECHUMINS ON THE CREED," 17

Daily Hymn

Daily Closing Prayer

Novena for Faith

Faith can be understood as "intellectual assent to truth" or as "immediate trust in God." Assenting to truth and trusting in God are two sides of the same theological coin. We do not trust that which we believe to be false. Perhaps faith is best understood as "the good habit of trusting in the truth that is God." This is a habit given to us, infused into us, by Truth himself. Exercising the virtue of faith builds its strength and leads us to eternal happiness. What does faith require? Not evidence or argument or experiment. Faith requires that we turn to God and acknowledge our dependence on him for everything we have and for everything we are and will become.

Opening Prayer

Gracious God, you made us to live with you and without you we cannot live. You infuse us with the good habit of trusting in your truth. With this faith we live and move and return to you—always loved, always forgiven. Build up in your people a lively faith; a powerful urge to seek you out; a determination to live in the world as righteous people; and make us true servants for the sake of your Son, Christ Jesus. In his name, we pray. Amen.

Scripture Reading

Now when Jesus came into the district of Caesarea Philippi, he asked his disciples, "Who do people say that the Son of Man is?" And they said, "Some say John the Baptist, but others Elijah, and still others Jeremiah or one of the prophets." He said to them, "But who do you say that I am?" Simon Peter answered, "You are the Messiah, the Son of the living God." And Jesus answered him, "Blessed are you, Simon son of Jonah! For flesh and blood has not revealed this to you, but my Father in heaven."

MATTHEW 16:13–17

Reading from Saint Basil the Great

Through the Holy Spirit comes our restoration to paradise, our ascension into the kingdom of heaven, our return to the adoption of sons, our liberty to call God our Father, our being made partakers of the grace of Christ, our being called children of light, our sharing in eternal glory, and, in a word, our being brought into a state of all "fullness of blessing," both in this world and in the world to come, of all the good gifts that are in store for us, by promise hereof, through faith, beholding the reflection of their grace as though they were already present, we await the full enjoyment. If such is the [guarantee], what the perfection? If such the first fruits, what the complete fulfilment?

"TREATISE ON THE HOLY SPIRIT"
(*DE SPIRITU SANCTO*), 15:36

Meditation

Saint Basil points out that through our faith we behold a reflection of the full enjoyment of all the promises God has made to us. He asks: if this reflection is merely the down payment on God's promise, then what must the payoff look like? Looking through my faith at the reflection of the full enjoyment of God's promises to me, what do I see? How do I use these promises to grow in holiness? How do I use the first fruits of God's gifts to me? (Remember: in biblical terms, "first fruits" were sacrificed or dedicated to God's service—first born, first harvest, first press of wine, etc.). For my faith, do I call God "Father"? Do I experience God as a loving, generous, guiding presence in my life? How do I partake in the graces/gifts won by Christ? In what sense am I an "adopted son"? God the Father revealed to Simon Peter that Jesus is the long-awaited Messiah. How is this revelation made to you today? How will you reveal it?

Closing Prayer

Trusting always in your infinite wisdom, Lord, I dedicate my life and work to your mission of bringing a fallen people back to your righteousness. But first I must learn to live more and more in the faith you have given me, trusting more and more in your providence: grant me the wisdom and courage I need to be the prophet and priest of the first fruits of faith; help me to discern your hand in my life and to accept with grace and dignity that my will is not always the best path to holiness. Keep me humble, wise, prudent, and blessed. In Christ's name we pray. Amen.

Novena for Hope

Opening Prayer

God of Hope, you are the goodness of your creation and all things you have created are good. From your perfection came everything that is, and to you all who love you will return. We do not live our lives as gambles against death but rather as living signs of your promises fulfilled in Christ Jesus. Transform our lives in the hope of life eternal. Send us out to bring hope to your world. In Christ's name we pray. Amen.

Scripture Reading

We know that the whole creation has been groaning in labour pains until now; and not only the creation, but we ourselves, who have the first fruits of the Spirit, groan inwardly while we wait for adoption, the redemption of our bodies. For in hope we were saved. Now hope that is seen is not hope. For who hopes for what is seen? But if we hope for what we do not see, we wait for it with patience.

ROMANS 8:22–25

Alternate

But we do not want you to be uninformed, brothers and sisters, about those who have died, so that you may not grieve as others do who have no hope. For since we believe that Jesus died and rose again, even so, through Jesus, God will bring with him those who have died. For this we declare to you by the word of the Lord, that we who are alive, who are left until the coming of the Lord, will by no means precede those who have died.

1 THESSALONIANS 4:13–15

Reading from *Spe Salvi*

In the same vein he says to the Thessalonians: you must not "grieve as others do who have no hope" (1 Th 4:13). Here too we see as a distinguishing mark of Christians the fact that they have a future: it is not that they know the details of what awaits them, but they know in general terms that their life will not end in emptiness. Only when the future is certain as a positive reality does it become possible to live the present as well. So now we can say: Christianity was not only "good news"—the communication of a hitherto unknown content. In our language we would say: the Christian message was not only "informative" but "performative". That means: the Gospel is not merely a communication of things that can be known—it is one that makes things happen and is life-changing. The dark door of time, of the future, has been thrown open. The one who has hope lives differently; the one who hopes has been granted the gift of a new life.

... So now we must ask explicitly: is the Christian faith also for us today a life-changing and life-sustaining hope?

Is it "performative" for us—is it a message which shapes our life in a new way, or is it just "information" which, in the meantime, we have set aside and which now seems to us to have been superseded by more recent information? ...

POPE BENEDICT XVI, *SPE SALVI*, 2, 10

Meditation

How do I understand the phrase "we are saved in hope"? How does hope save me? From what does hope save me? For what reason am I saved? How does hope throw open "the dark door of time"? I have been granted new life in hope. How does hope give me new life? How do I live in hope so as to demonstrate that my life is new?

Have I set aside the gospel proclamation of hope in favor of some other hope—a medical hope, a technological hope, some material hope such as wealth or power? Do I understand my hope in Christ as something I must perform in order to live, or do I understand this hope as mere information to be studied?

Closing Prayer

God of Hope, truly, we are saved by your love for us. Created to receive all that we are from you, we long to be perfected in your image. Though we will die in this world, we know our lives will be glorified with you in heaven. We live in hope. Not the hope of chance or the hope of material excellence, but the hope we have when we trust in your Word, Christ Jesus. Bring us to you as we wait with endurance. In Christ's name we pray. Amen.

Novena for Love

In December of 2005, our Holy Father, Pope Benedict XVI, published his first encyclical, *Deus Caritas Est*, or "God is Love." In this letter to the Church, Pope Benedict teaches us that our lives in faith are more than an intellectual/emotive assent to the plot of a spiritual story or theological argument. He writes: "Being Christian is not the result of an ethical choice or a lofty idea, but the encounter with an event, a person, which gives life a new horizon and a decisive direction" (*DCE* 1). The event, the person is the coming of the embodiment of Love in the person of Jesus Christ among us.

Opening Prayer

Lord of Charity, in love you created us to love so that we might return to you fully loving. Though we often fail to love you and one another as we ought, and even though we love in ways that will not satisfy, we always feel the need to love. We recognize this as a passionate gift that draws us together and toward you. Help us to order rightly the passion to love; help to see our end in love; help us to love others as a sign of your love for us. In Christ's name we pray. Amen.

Scripture Reading

Beloved, let us love one another, because love is from God; everyone who loves is born of God and knows God. Whoever does not love does not know God, for God is love. God's love was revealed among us in this way: God sent his only Son into the world so that we might live through him. In this is love, not that we loved God but that he loved us and sent his Son to be the atoning sacrifice for our sins. Beloved, since God loved us so much, we also ought to love one another. No one has ever seen God; if we love one another, God lives in us, and his love is perfected in us.

By this we know that we abide in him and he in us, because he has given us of his Spirit.

1 JOHN 4:7–13

Reading from *Deus Caritas Est*

The unbreakable bond between love of God and love of neighbour is emphasized. One is so closely connected to the other that to say that we love God becomes a lie if we are closed to our neighbour or hate him altogether. Saint John's words should rather be interpreted to mean that love of neighbour is a path that leads to the encounter with God, and that closing our eyes to our neighbour also blinds us to God.

True, no one has ever seen God as he is. And yet God is not totally invisible to us; he does not remain completely inaccessible. God loved us first, ... and this love of God has appeared in our midst. He has become visible in as much as he "has sent his only Son into the world, so that we might live through him" (1 Jn 4:9). God has made himself visible: in Jesus we are able to see the Father (Jn 14:9). Indeed, God is visible in a number of ways. In the love-story recounted by the Bible, he comes towards us, he seeks to win our hearts, all the way to the Last Supper, to the piercing of his heart on the Cross, to his appearances after the Resurrection and to the great deeds by which, through the activity of the Apostles, he guided the nascent Church along its path....He has loved us first and he continues to do so; we too, then, can respond with love. God does not demand of us a feeling which we ourselves are incapable of producing. He loves us, he makes us see and experience his love, and since he has "loved us first," love can also blossom as a response within us.

POPE BENEDICT XVI, *DEUS CARITAS EST*, 16, 17

Meditation

In our consumerist culture love is too often portrayed in sexual terms, or in terms better suited to sentimental poetry. Whether expressed in purely physical terms or in terms of sugary sentiment, love prevails as a passion that compels us to seek out one another for intimacy—friendships, romantic relationships, even the misguided one-night stand. What does it mean for me to be loved by Love himself? In what concrete ways do I see/feel/hear this love for me? How do I return his love? In what ways have I or do I misplace love or use it in a disordered fashion? Do I see love as a habit that will lead me to holiness? John tells us that God's love for us is most fully revealed in Christ. How do I see Christ as the revelation of God's love for me? How do I love others in obedience to Christ's command to love?

Closing Prayer

Loving and merciful Father, you sent your Son among us as a living sign of your love for all creation. He died on the cross as our friend to save us from final death. You raised him from the grave as another sign to us of how much you love. Help us to discern the path of love to you. Help us to love as we ought. Keep us rightly directed, steadfast and true, holy and complete in your love. In his name we pray. Amen.

Novena of the Lord's Prayer

When the disciples asked their Lord to teach them to pray, he prayed what we now call the "Our Father." This prayer is the template for all Christian prayer in that it contains every petition necessary for one's growth in holiness. By acknowledging God as Father, we place ourselves in humble submission to his abundance and generosity, asking not only for our daily physical needs but also for our spiritual nourishment. The readings for this novena are taken from Cyprian of Carthage's reflections on the Lord's Prayer written between 246–258 AD.

Daily Opening Prayer

Lord, as your faithful child, I lift my hands in need, asking you with all my heart and soul to give them everything I need to grow closer to you in holiness. Heeding the words of my savior, Jesus Christ, I know that a hungry stomach and a cold body cannot properly hear your Word spoken. Therefore, I ask as well that you give me everything I need to sustain myself in mind and body. With humble thanks and praise for these gifts, I glorify your name, O Lord, knowing that everything I am and will be belongs to you and you alone. In Christ's name I pray. Amen.

READINGS BY DAY

DAY ONE

Before all things, the Teacher of peace and the Master of unity would not have prayer to be made singly and individually, as for one who prays to pray for himself alone. For we say not "My Father, which art in heaven," nor "Give me this day my daily bread;" nor does each one ask that only his own debt should be forgiven him; nor does he request for himself alone that he may not be led into temptation, and delivered from evil. Our prayer is public and common; and when we pray, we pray not for one, but for the whole people, because we the whole people are one. The God of peace and the Teacher of concord, who taught unity, willed that one should thus pray for all, even as He Himself bore us all in one.

"ON THE LORD'S PRAYER," 8

DAY TWO

But what matters of deep moment are contained in the Lord's prayer! How many and! How great, briefly collected in the words, but spiritually abundant in virtue! so that there is absolutely nothing passed over that is not comprehended in these our prayers and petitions, as in a compendium of heavenly doctrine. "After this manner," says He, "pray ye: Our Father, which art in heaven." The new man, born again and restored to his God by His grace, says "Father," in the first place because he has now begun to be a son. "He came," He says, "to His own, and His own received Him not. But as many as received Him, to them gave He power to become the sons of God, even to them that believe in His name." The man, therefore, who has believed in His name, and has become God's son, ought from this point to begin both to give thanks and to profess himself God's son, by declaring that God is his Father in heaven; and also to bear witness, among the very first words of his new birth, that he has renounced an earthly and carnal father, and that he has begun to know as well as to have as a father Him only who is in heaven…

"ON THE LORD'S PRAYER," 9

DAY THREE

After this we say, "Hallowed be Thy name;" not that we wish for God that He may be hallowed by our prayers, but that we beseech of Him that His name may be hallowed in us. But by whom is God sanctified, since He Himself sanctifies? Well, because He says, "Be ye holy, even as I am holy," we ask and entreat, that we who were sanctified in baptism may continue in that which we have begun to be. And this we daily pray for; for we have need of daily sanctification, that we who daily fall away may wash out our sins by continual sanctification. And what the sanctification is which is conferred upon us by the condescension of God, the apostle declares, when he says, "neither fornicators, nor idolaters, nor adulterers, nor effeminate, nor abusers of themselves with mankind, nor thieves, nor deceivers, nor drunkards, nor revilers, nor extortioners, shall inherit the kingdom of God. And such indeed were you; but ye are washed; but ye are justified; but ye are sanctified in the name of our Lord Jesus Christ, and by the Spirit of our God."

"ON THE LORD'S PRAYER," 12

DAY FOUR

There follows in the prayer, Thy kingdom come. We ask that the kingdom of God may be set forth to us, even as we also ask that His name may be sanctified in us. For when does God not reign, or when does that begin with Him which both always has been, and never ceases to be? We pray that our kingdom, which has been promised us by God, may come, which was acquired by the blood and passion of Christ; that we who first are His subjects in the world, may hereafter reign with Christ when He reigns, as He Himself promises and says, "Come, ye blessed of my Father, receive the kingdom which has been prepared for you from the beginning of the world." Christ Himself, dearest brethren, however, may be the kingdom of God, whom we day by day desire to come, whose advent we crave to be quickly manifested to us. For since He is Himself the Resurrection, since in Him we rise again, so also the kingdom of God may be understood to be Himself, since in Him we shall reign. But we do well in seeking the kingdom of God, that is, the heavenly kingdom, because there is also an earthly kingdom.

ON THE LORD'S PRAYER, 13

DAY FIVE

We add, also, and say, "Thy will be done, as in heaven so in earth;" not that God should do what He wills, but that we may be able to do what God wills. For who resists God, that He may not do what He wills? But since we are hindered by the devil from obeying with our thought and deed God's will in all things, we pray and ask that God's will may be done in us; and that it may be done in us we have need of God's good will, that is, of His help and protection, since no one is strong in his own strength, but he is safe by the grace and mercy of God. And further, the Lord, setting forth the infirmity of the humanity which He bore, says, "Father, if it be possible, let this cup pass from me'" and affording an example to His disciples that they should do not their own will, but God's...

"ON THE LORD'S PRAYER," 14

DAY SIX

As the prayer goes forward, we ask and say, "Give us this day our daily bread." And this may be understood both spiritually and literally, because either way of understanding it is rich in divine usefulness to our salvation. For Christ is the bread of life; and this bread does not belong to all men, but it is ours. And according as we say, "Our Father," because He is the Father of those who understand and believe; so also we call it "our bread," because

Christ is the bread of those who are in union with His body. And we ask that this bread should be given to us daily, that we who are in Christ, and daily receive the Eucharist for the food of salvation, may not, by the interposition of some heinous sin, by being prevented, as withheld and not communicating, from partaking of the heavenly bread, be separated from Christ's body, as He Himself predicts, and warns, "I am the bread of life which came down from heaven. If any man eat of my bread, he shall live for ever: and the bread which I will give is my flesh, for the life of the world."...And therefore we ask that our bread—that is, Christ—may be given to us daily, that we who abide and live in Christ may not depart from His sanctification and body.

"ON THE LORD'S PRAYER," 18

DAY SEVEN

After this we also entreat for our sins, saying, "And forgive us our debts, as we also forgive our debtors." After the supply of food, pardon of sin is also asked for, that he who is fed by God may live in God, and that not only the present and temporal life may be provided for, but the eternal also, to which we may come if our sins are forgiven; and these the Lord calls debts, as He says in His Gospel, "I forgave thee all that debt, because thou desiredst me." And how necessarily, how providently and salutarily, are we admonished that we are sinners, since we are compelled to entreat for our sins, and while pardon is asked for from God, the soul recalls its own consciousness of sin! Lest any one should flatter himself that he is innocent, and by exalting himself should more deeply perish, he is instructed and taught that he sins daily, in that he is bidden to entreat daily for his sins.

"ON THE LORD'S PRAYER," 22

DAY EIGHT

Moreover, the Lord of necessity admonishes us to say in prayer, "And suffer us not to be led into temptation." In which words it is shown that the adversary can do nothing against us except God shall have previously permitted it; so that all our fear, and devotion, and obedience may be turned towards God, since in our temptations nothing is permitted to evil unless power is given from Him. This is proved by divine Scripture, which says, "Nebuchadnezzar king of Babylon came to Jerusalem, and besieged it; and the Lord delivered it into his hand." But power is given to evil against us according to our sins, as it is written, "Who gave Jacob for a spoil, and Israel to those who make a prey of Him? Did not the Lord, against whom they sinned, and would not walk in His ways, nor hear His law? and He has brought upon them the anger of His wrath."...

"ON THE LORD'S PRAYER," 25

DAY NINE

After all these things, in the conclusion of the prayer comes a brief clause, which shortly and comprehensively sums up all our petitions and our prayers. For we conclude by saying, "But deliver us from evil," comprehending all adverse things which the enemy attempts against us in this world, from which there may be a faithful and sure protection if God deliver us, if He afford His help to us who pray for and implore it. And when we say, Deliver us from evil, there remains nothing further which ought to be asked. When we have once asked for God's protection against evil, and have obtained it, then against everything which the devil and the world work against us we stand secure and safe. For what fear is there in this life, to the man whose guardian in this life is God?

"ON THE LORD'S PRAYER," 27

Daily Prayer: Our Father

Daily Closing Prayer

Lord God, may your name be blessed in me as I live this day. May your wisdom and love be on my lips and in hands as I meet those who suffer most. Give me the courage and strength I require to be both your humble child and mighty preacher. Burn away my sins as you look on the faith of your Church; hold me closer to the heart of your Son; and keep me on your narrow way. In Christ's name I pray. Amen.

Psalm Novena for Growth in Holiness

As imperfect creatures perfectly loved by our Creator, we are relentlessly pulled toward our perfection in Christ. When we freely cooperate with the graces God has given us, we grow in holiness, that is, we become more and more like Christ who is fully human, fully divine. This novena will help you move through nine days of reflection on sin, repentance, contrition, joy, and then gratitude for God's mercy.

Opening Prayer

Gracious and merciful Father, as a child of your beloved family, I come to you conscious of my failures, my joys, my disappointments, and my many loves. With all that I am and with all that I have to give, I place myself, wholly and freely, in your care and ask you to show me the stumbling blocks on my path to holiness. Show me the temptations, the vices, the disordered passions, the follies of sin that detain me. Show me all those people in my life who obstruct me in my journey to your perfection; all those you send to assist me; and all of those to whom you send me as an angel. Show me the way around the obstacles, through the temptations, over the vices, and on to you, my Lord and Savior.

Spirit of Love and Mercy, be with me as I pray this novena. Show me my faults, my strengths, my challenges, and my gifts. Help me to be your perfect servant. In Jesus' holy name, I pray. Amen.

DAY ONE: MERCY

Even before you contemplate contrition and repentance, you must acknowledge the overwhelming presence of God's freely given mercy. You are able to bring your contrite heart to the Lord precisely because he has granted you the grace of his mercy.

Opening Prayer

O give thanks to the Lord, for he is good,
*   for his steadfast love endures for ever.*
give thanks to the God of gods,
*   for his steadfast love endures for ever.*
give thanks to the Lord of lords,
*   for his steadfast love endures for ever;*

who alone does great wonders,
*   for his steadfast love endures for ever;*
who by understanding made the heavens,
*   for his steadfast love endures for ever;*
who spread out the earth on the waters,
*   for his steadfast love endures for ever;*
who made the great lights,
*   for his steadfast love endures for ever;*
the sun to rule over the day,
*   for his steadfast love endures for ever;*
the moon and stars to rule over the night,
*   for his steadfast love endures for ever;*

It is he who remembered us in our low estate,
*   for his steadfast love endures for ever;*
and rescued us from our foes,
*   for his steadfast love endures for ever;*
who gives food to all flesh,
*   for his steadfast love endures for ever.*

O give thanks to the God of heaven,
*   for his steadfast love endures for ever.*

PSALM 136:1–9, 23–26

Meditation: How have I received God's gift of mercy? How have I shown mercy to others?

Pray: Lord of mercy, I give you thanks and praise for your compassion. Without your loving kindness, I could not grow in holiness; there would be no path for me to travel to you. With gratitude, I receive all you have to give me. Keep me on your way of mercy, Father. I ask this in Jesus' holy name. Amen.

DAY TWO: TRUST

Having acknowledged God's mercy, you next move to the virtue of faith, that is, the good habit of trusting in God's promise of compassion and forgiveness.

Opening Prayer

Happy are those whose transgression is forgiven,
whose sin is covered.
Happy are those to whom the Lord imputes no iniquity,
and in whose spirit there is no deceit.

While I kept silence, my body wasted away
through my groaning all day long.
For day and night your hand was heavy upon me;
my strength was dried up as by the heat of summer.

Then I acknowledged my sin to you,
and I did not hide my iniquity;
I said, I will confess my transgressions to the Lord,
and you forgave the guilt of my sin.

Therefore let all who are faithful
     offer prayer to you;
at a time of distress, the rush of mighty waters
     shall not reach them.
You are a hiding-place for me;
     you preserve me from trouble;
     you surround me with glad cries of deliverance.

I will instruct you and teach you the way you should go;
     I will counsel you with my eye upon you.
Do not be like a horse or a mule, without understanding,
     whose temper must be curbed with bit and bridle,
     else it will not stay near you.

Many are the torments of the wicked,
     but steadfast love surrounds those who trust in the Lord.
Be glad in the Lord and rejoice, O righteous,
     and shout for joy, all you upright in heart.

PSALM 32

Meditation: How do I show the Lord that I trust him?

Pray: Lord God, I give you thanks and praise for your trust in me. Without your gift of faith, I could not grow in holiness; there would be no path for me to travel to you. With gratitude, and trusting fully in the goodness of your will for me, I receive all the blessings you have to give me. Keep me on the trusting way, Father. I ask this in Jesus' holy name. Amen.

DAY THREE: CONTRITION

With mercy and trust as your firm foundation, you are ready to examine your conscience and express your contrition for any offense you may have given to God, to his Church, or to one of your neighbors. Heart-felt sorrow for sin is a sign of a willingness to be obedient, that is, to listen to the Lord.

Opening Prayer

Have mercy on me, O God,
*   according to your steadfast love;*
according to your abundant mercy
*   blot out my transgressions.*
Wash me thoroughly from my iniquity,
*   and cleanse me from my sin.*

For I know my transgressions,
*   and my sin is ever before me.*
Against you, you alone, have I sinned,
*   and done what is evil in your sight,*
so that you are justified in your sentence
*   and blameless when you pass judgement.*
Indeed, I was born guilty,
*   a sinner when my mother conceived me.*

You desire truth in the inward being;
*   therefore teach me wisdom in my secret heart.*
Purge me with hyssop, and I shall be clean;
*   wash me, and I shall be whiter than snow.*
Let me hear joy and gladness;
*   let the bones that you have crushed rejoice.*
Hide your face from my sins,
*   and blot out all my iniquities.*

Create in me a clean heart, O God,
and put a new and right spirit within me.
Do not cast me away from your presence,
and do not take your holy spirit from me.
Restore to me the joy of your salvation,
and sustain in me a willing spirit.

PSALM 51:3–14

Meditation: For what faults/sins am I contrite? What are the vices that trip me up on the way to holiness?

Pray: Good and gracious God, I give you thanks and praise for granting me a contrite heart. Without your forgiveness, I could not grow in holiness; there would be no path for me to travel to you. With deepest sorrow, I repent of all my sins; with deepest desire, I long to please you. In gratitude, I receive all the gifts of contrition you have to give me. Keep me on your way of repentance, Father. I ask this in Jesus' holy name. Amen.

DAY FOUR: REDEDICATION

A truly contrite heart cleaned in God's mercy is easily re-dedicated to his service. You are called upon this day to set aside any idols that replace the Lord as your only spiritual focus.

Opening Prayer
Protect me, O God, for in you I take refuge.
I say to the Lord, You are my Lord;
I have no good apart from you.

As for the holy ones in the land, they are the noble,
in whom is all my delight.

Those who choose another god multiply their sorrows;
　　their drink-offerings of blood I will not pour out
　　or take their names upon my lips.

The Lord is my chosen portion and my cup;
　　you hold my lot.
The boundary lines have fallen for me in pleasant places;
　　I have a goodly heritage.

I bless the Lord who gives me counsel;
　　in the night also my heart instructs me.
I keep the Lord always before me;
　　because he is at my right hand, I shall not be moved.

Therefore my heart is glad, and my soul rejoices;
　　my body also rests secure.
For you do not give me up to Sheol,
　　or let your faithful one see the Pit.

You show me the path of life.
　　In your presence there is fullness of joy;
　　in your right hand are pleasures for evermore.

PSALM 16

Meditation: How will I re-dedicate my life to the Lord's service today? What "idols" do I need to remove from my "household"?

Pray: Lord of lords, I give you thanks and praise for your majesty and power. Without your abundant generosity, I could not grow in holiness; there would be no path for me to travel to you. With unshaken resolve, I rededicate myself to your service alone, receiving all you have to give to me on this path. Keep on your way of fidelity, Father. I ask this in Jesus' holy name. Amen.

DAY FIVE: WORSHIP!

In the simplest terms, worship is our recognition and celebration of our creaturely natures, that is, when we worship we direct our full attention—body, soul, mind—to the one Creator and freely admit that we his creatures.

Opening Prayer

O Lord, our Sovereign,
how majestic is your name in all the earth!

You have set your glory above the heavens.
Out of the mouths of babes and infants
you have founded a bulwark because of your foes,
to silence the enemy and the avenger.

When I look at your heavens, the work of your fingers,
the moon and the stars that you have established;
what are human beings that you are mindful of them,
mortals that you care for them?

Yet you have made them a little lower than God,
and crowned them with glory and honour.
You have given them dominion over the works of your hands;
you have put all things under their feet,
all sheep and oxen,
and also the beasts of the field,
the birds of the air, and the fish of the sea,
whatever passes along the paths of the seas.

O Lord, our Sovereign,
how majestic is your name in all the earth!

PSALM 8

Meditation: Having received the Lord's mercy and rededicated myself to his service, how will I offer him the worship that is his due?

Pray: Awesome and wondrous Lord, I adore you and give your praise! Without your glory shining out to all creation, I could not grow in holiness; there would be no path for me to travel to you. With my mind freed and my heart adoring, I receive all you have to give me that I may honor you more fully. Keep me on your way of adoration, Father. I ask this in Jesus' holy name. Amen.

DAY SIX: HUMILITY

In offering God our worship, we are admitting to our total dependence on him for our very being. By acknowledging that we are "dust," we strenghten the bond of gratitude we have with God and grow in humility.

Opening Prayer

Incline your ear, O Lord, and answer me,
*   for I am poor and needy.*
Preserve my life, for I am devoted to you;
*   save your servant who trusts in you.*
You are my God; be gracious to me, O Lord,
*   for to you do I cry all day long.*
Gladden the soul of your servant,
*   for to you, O Lord, I lift up my soul.*
For you, O Lord, are good and forgiving,
*   abounding in steadfast love to all who call on you.*
Give ear, O Lord, to my prayer;
*   listen to my cry of supplication.*

In the day of my trouble I call on you,
for you will answer me.

There is none like you among the gods, O Lord,
nor are there any works like yours.
All the nations you have made shall come
and bow down before you, O Lord,
and shall glorify your name.
For you are great and do wondrous things;
you alone are God.
Teach me your way, O Lord,
that I may walk in your truth;
give me an undivided heart to revere your name.
I give thanks to you, O Lord my God, with my whole heart,
and I will glorify your name for ever.
For great is your steadfast love towards me;
you have delivered my soul from the depths of Sheol.

PSALM 86:1–13

Meditation: How am I completely dependent on my God for everything I have and everything I am? In what areas of my life do I need to grow in humility?

Pray: Creator God, I give you thanks and praise for my very existence. Without your Word spoken over the void, nothing in creation would exist. There would be no path, no travelers, no humble way to walk. With gratitude, I receive the gift of my very being and give you praise for your creation. Remembering that I am dust and to dust I will return, in all humility, I lift my prayers with thanksgiving. Keep me on your way of humility, Father. I ask this in Jesus' holy name. Amen.

DAY SEVEN: TAKING REFUGE

How often do we rush to fix our problems without first asking God for this help? If we are truly humble, that is, fully aware of our dependence on God, we turn first to him for our comfort and refuge.

Opening Prayer

To the leader. Of David.
In the Lord I take refuge; how can you say to me,
'Flee like a bird to the mountains;
for look, the wicked bend the bow,
they have fitted their arrow to the string,
to shoot in the dark at the upright in heart.
If the foundations are destroyed,
what can the righteous do?'

The Lord is in his holy temple;
the Lord's throne is in heaven.
His eyes behold, his gaze examines humankind.
The Lord tests the righteous and the wicked,
and his soul hates the lover of violence.
On the wicked he will rain coals of fire and sulphur;
a scorching wind shall be the portion of their cup.
For the Lord is righteous;
he loves righteous deeds;
the upright shall behold his face.

PSALM 11

Meditation: In times of temptation and trouble, do I run to the Lord and take refuge? Or do I try to handle these troubles on my own? How can I run faster to the Lord for protection when the enemy is prepared to strike?

Pray: Refuge of sinners, I give you thanks and praise for your protection. Without your invincible strength, I could not grow resist the enemy's traps; there would be no safe path for me to travel to you. With gratitude, I receive the help of your strong right hand and take swift refuge under your mighty wings. Keep me on your way of refuge, Father. I ask this in Jesus' holy name. Amen.

DAY EIGHT: FRIENDSHIP

Though we are the Lord's servants, we are also his friends in Christ Jesus, the friends for whom he died on the cross. Our friendship with God, though necessarily unequal, is a relationship bound in true affection and sacrifice. If you doubt this, look at a crucifix.

Opening Prayer

My God, my God, why have you forsaken me?
   Why are you so far from helping me
      from the words of my groaning?
O my God, I cry by day, but you do not answer;
   and by night, but find no rest.

Yet you are holy,
   enthroned on the praises of Israel.
In you our ancestors trusted;
   they trusted, and you delivered them.
To you they cried, and were saved;
   in you they trusted, and were not put to shame.

But I am a worm, and not human;
   scorned by others, and despised by the people.

All who see me mock at me;
*   they make mouths at me, they shake their heads;*
'Commit your cause to the Lord; let him deliver—
*   let him rescue the one in whom he delights!'*

Yet it was you who took me from the womb;
*   you kept me safe on my mother's breast.*
On you I was cast from my birth,
*   and since my mother bore me you have been my God.*
Do not be far from me,
*   for trouble is near*
*   and there is no one to help.*

PSALM 22:1–11

Meditation: Having taken refuge under the strong right hand of God, why do I despair? Why do I sometimes feel abandoned? What does it mean to me to say that God is my friend?

Pray: My Lord since my birth, I give you thanks and praise for your friendship. Without your constant rescue, I could not grow in holiness; there would be no friendly path for me to travel to you. With gratitude, I receive your friendship, your holy company. Keep me on your way of friendship, Father. I ask this in Jesus' holy name. Amen.

DAY NINE: REJOICE AND SING!

One of the surest ways we have of growing in holiness is giving God praise, thanksgiving and rejoicing in his presence. This last day of the novena is best spent singing, laughing, and enjoying God's company and the company of good friends.

Opening Prayer

O sing to the Lord a new song;
*   sing to the Lord, all the earth.*
Sing to the Lord, bless his name;
*   tell of his salvation from day to day.*
Declare his glory among the nations,
*   his marvellous works among all the peoples.*
For great is the Lord, and greatly to be praised;
*   he is to be revered above all gods.*
For all the gods of the peoples are idols,
*   but the Lord made the heavens.*
Honour and majesty are before him;
*   strength and beauty are in his sanctuary.*

Ascribe to the Lord, O families of the peoples,
*   ascribe to the Lord glory and strength.*
Ascribe to the Lord the glory due his name;
*   bring an offering, and come into his courts.*
Worship the Lord in holy splendour;
*   tremble before him, all the earth.*

Say among the nations, The Lord is king!
*   The world is firmly established; it shall never be moved.*
*   He will judge the peoples with equity.*
Let the heavens be glad, and let the earth rejoice;
*   let the sea roar, and all that fills it;*
*   let the field exult, and everything in it.*
Then shall all the trees of the forest sing for joy
*   before the Lord; for he is coming,*
*   for he is coming to judge the earth.*
He will judge the world with righteousness,
*   and the peoples with his truth.*

PSALM 96

Meditation: What new song can I sing to the Lord today? What new service can I provide for his Church? What new mercy, new forgiveness, new love can I show the world as a witness to God mercy and love?

Pray: Lord of joy and song, I sing your praises and rejoice in thanksgiving that you are my God. Without the music of your graces, I could not sing to you in adoration; there would be no strings, no lutes, no drums, no voices raised in celebration! With my heart pounding to the beat of your will for me and my soul reading the notes of your love, I receive now all the music, all the songs, all the rejoicing you have to give. Keep me on your way of praise, Father. I ask this in Jesus' holy name. Amen.

Novena of the Four Dominican Pillars

Opening Prayer (for all nine days):
Lord, in obedience to your Word and trusting in your promises to bring us to you in your perfection, we pray that you grant us the wisdom, patience, and fortitude to carry out our vows as living witnesses of your Gospel. In our study, prayer, community life, and ministry, may we be the spark that sets the world on fire with your Holy Spirit, teaching and preaching all that our Lord taught and preached. In his holy name we pray. Amen.

DAY ONE: BRING GOOD TIDINGS

Opening Prayer

How beautiful upon the mountains
*   are the feet of the messenger who announces peace,*
who brings good news,
*   who announces salvation,*
*   who says to Zion, Your God reigns.*
Listen! Your sentinels lift up their voices,
*   together they sing for joy;*
for in plain sight they see
*   the return of the Lord to Zion.*
Break forth together into singing,
*   you ruins of Jerusalem;*
for the Lord has comforted his people,
*   he has redeemed Jerusalem.*
The Lord has bared his holy arm
*   before the eyes of all the nations;*
and all the ends of the earth shall see
*   the salvation of our God.*

ISAIAH 52:7–10

Meditation: Where will my "beautiful feet" take me today to announce the glad tidings of the Lord? How will I announce this saving message? How does my community (family, friends, neighbors) help or hinder me in this announcement?

DAY TWO: STUDY THE WISDOM OF THE FOOL

Opening Prayer

Do you not know that you are God's temple and that God's Spirit dwells in you? If anyone destroys God's temple, God will destroy that person. For God's temple is holy, and you are that temple.

Do not deceive yourselves. If you think that you are wise in this age, you should become fools so that you may become wise. For the wisdom of this world is foolishness with God. For it is written,

"He catches the wise in their craftiness,"

and again,

"The Lord knows the thoughts of the wise,
    that they are futile."

So let no one boast about human leaders. For all things are yours, whether Paul or Apollos or Cephas or the world or life or death or the present or the future—all belong to you, and you belong to Christ, and Christ belongs to God.

1 CORINTHIANS 3:16–23

Meditation: Why do I study (read, write, reflect)? What do I study? How does my study help me to become "foolish"? How am I tempted by the "wise of this age" to see God's wisdom as foolishness? How does study help/hinder my witness to the Gospel?

Pray: Spirit of God, you made us to be your holy temples. You send us out to be walking tabernacles of your presence in the world. Though we are often seduced by the false wisdom of the world we walk, we trust in your mercy to bring us back to you. All belongs to you. In my study and prayer, elevate your eternal wisdom so that I may see the truth of both heaven and earth. Keep me diligent against the temptations of any philosophies that would lead me away from you. And keep me always open to the truth I seek. Amen.

DAY THREE: COMMUNITY AS FRIENDSHIP

Opening Prayer

The Dominican tradition of community is deeply marked by how we understand our relationship with God. In the Church there are two major traditions. One sees our relationship with God in spousal terms, the love of the Bridegroom and the Bride. The other sees it in terms of friendship. Both are found in the Order, but we have especially kept alive the Johannine theology of friendship, which has often been neglected. For St Thomas Aquinas, the heart of God's life was the friendship of the Father and the Son, which is the Holy Spirit. In the Spirit we are God's friends. And so praying is talking to God as to a friend. According to Carranza, a sixteenth century Spanish Dominican, prayer is "conversing familiarly with God....discussing all your affairs with God, whether they are exalted or lowly, of heaven or of earth, to do with the soul or to do with the body, great or small; it is to open your heart to him and pour yourself out entirely before him, leaving nothing hidden; it is to tell him your labours, your sins, your desires, and all the rest, everything that is in your soul, and to relax with him as one friend relaxes with another."

FATHER TIMOTHY RADCLIFFE, OP
" 'A CITY SET ON A HILLTOP CANNOT BE HIDDEN':
A CONTEMPLATIVE LIFE," 2001

Meditation: How would I describe my prayer life to someone who has never heard of prayer? In what way am I God's friend? How does my prayer life exemplify this friendship? Am I able to relax in the presence of God and tell him everything that is in my soul? Does this practice of prayer extend to my community/family?

Pray: Lord God, friend of all, you first created us from nothing; you gave us the law and the prophets; you promised us eternal life with you. You sent us your Son to be our teacher and friend. Instill in me a longing for Christ's friendship. Infuse me with the desire for holy companions, the company of the saints. With them, show me how to relax in your presence and trust in your care. Amen.

DAY FOUR: ALL THINGS IN COMMON

Opening Prayer

Peter said to them, "Repent, and be baptized every one of you in the name of Jesus Christ so that your sins may be forgiven; and you will receive the gift of the Holy Spirit. For the promise is for you, for your children, and for all who are far away, everyone whom the Lord our God calls to him." And he testified with many other arguments and exhorted them, saying, "Save yourselves from this corrupt generation." So those who welcomed his message were baptized, and that day about three thousand persons were added. They devoted themselves to the apostles' teaching and fellowship, to the breaking of bread and the prayers.

Awe came upon everyone, because many wonders and signs were being done by the apostles. All who believed were together and had all things in common; they would sell their possessions and goods and distribute the proceeds to all, as any had need. Day by day, as they spent much time together in the temple, they broke bread at home and ate their food with glad and generous hearts, praising God and having the goodwill of all the people. And day by day the Lord added to their number those who were being saved.

ACTS 2:38–47

Meditation: Am I able to distinguish between my wants and my needs? What/who encourages me to turn my wants into needs? When praying about my needs, how do I approach God—am I humble, entitled, indifferent, anxious, fearful, joyous? In what way do I share my graced bounty with others in my community? In what way do I share daily in the life of my community? Am I part of a "corrupt generation"? If so, how do I challenge those around me to seek out holiness in Christ? How do I challenge any corruption that might seek to influence my own pursuit of holiness? Am I a corrupt influence?

Pray: Lord, the Church received the gift of your Holy Spirit at Pentecost. Devoting herself to the teaching of the Apostles, prayer, and the breaking of bread, your Church became a living Body, a society of compassion. Help me to put aside my selfish wants; to detach myself from the temptations of possessions; to surrender my prideful will. Give me to the strength and courage to challenge corruption and the wisdom to do so with charity. Amen.

DAY FIVE: STUDY IS AN ACT OF HOPE

Opening Prayer

When St. Dominic wandered through the south of France, his life in danger, he used to sing cheerfully. "He always appeared cheerful and happy, except when he was moved by compassion for any trouble which afflicted his neighbour." And this joy of Dominic is inseparable from our vocation to be preachers of the good news. We are called to "give an account of the hope that is within us" (I Peter 3:15). Today, in a world crucified by suffering, violence and poverty, our vocation is both harder and more necessary than ever. There is a crisis of hope in every part of the world. How are we to live Dominic's joy when we are people of our time, and we share the crises of our peoples and the strengths and weaknesses of our culture? How can we nurture a deep hope, grounded in God's unshakable promise of life and happiness for his children?...To study is itself an act of hope, since it expresses our confidence that there is a meaning to our lives and the sufferings of our people. And this meaning comes to us as a gift, a Word of Hope promising life.

FATHER TIMOTHY RADCLIFFE, OP
"THE WELLSPRING OF HOPE STUDY
AND THE ANNUNCIATION OF THE GOOD NEWS," 1996

Meditation: Do I consistently give an account of the hope that is within me? In my studies, do I approach the material I am learning as a means of preaching/witnessing to the hope I share with the Church in God's promises? How do I share in the crises of those around me? In what way do my studies assist me in living with the despair and longing of others and at the same time help me to help them and to be helped in turn? If hope is the good habit of living God's promises right now, how am I an assiduous student of hope; that is, how have I made myself a disciple of hope in my studies?

Pray: God of hope, you have fulfilled your promise to send to us a Messiah. In Christ Jesus, you yourself came to us and showed us a way home. We worship you as our faithful Lord, constant and unswerving in your love for us. Make me a living sign of this hope. Make me an instrument for showing forth the fulfillment of your promises in Christ. Give me all I need to be hope in a world of suffering, to be your prophet and priest of life everlasting. Amen.

DAY SIX: PRAYER IS THE WORD ALIVE IN US

Opening Prayer

In contemplation, we turn our whole attention to God. But there is something else as well. God's Word, though utterly transcendent in its source, has come down into the world, and has taken flesh. "God", as Simone Weil once remarked, has to be on the side of the subject." The initiative is always his. Accordingly, both in our work and in our prayer, we come to realize that Christ is not just the object of our regard. He is the Word alive within us, the friend "in whom we live and move and have our being". And thus, we can make bold to say, echoing the First Letter of St. John: This is contemplation - this is contemplative love - not so much that we contemplate God, but that God has first contemplated us, and that now in us, in some sense, and even through us, as part of the mystery of his risen life in the Church, he contemplates the world.

FATHER PAUL MURRAY, OP
"RECOVERING THE CONTEMPLATIVE DIMENSION," 2001

Meditation: If I am able to love because God first loved me, and if I am able to contemplate God because he first contemplated me, then how do I understand the idea that the Word is alive within me? How do I live according to this Word? How do I allow this Word to teach me, lead me, challenge me? If God's Word—in Scripture, through creation, and as Christ Jesus—is "within me," how do I send the Word out into the world so that it might be heard? Do I sometimes impede others from hearing the Word? How so?

Pray: Lord God, truly, in you we live and move and have our being. Your Word is alive in us—thriving, growing, spreading—transforming a fallen creation into the new heavens and the new earth. That I may better contemplate your Word within me, help me to quiet my soul—to bring my mind to peace, my heart to rest. Amen.

DAY SEVEN: SHARING IN THE GOSPEL

Opening Prayer

If I proclaim the gospel, this gives me no ground for boasting, for an obligation is laid on me, and woe betide me if I do not proclaim the gospel! For if I do this of my own will, I have a reward; but if not of my own will, I am entrusted with a commission. What then is my reward? Just this: that in my proclamation I may make the gospel free of charge, so as not to make full use of my rights in the gospel.

For though I am free with respect to all, I have made myself a slave to all, so that I might win more of them. To the Jews I became as a Jew, in order to win Jews. To those under the law I became as one under the law (though I myself am not under the law) so that I might win those under the law. To those outside the law I became as one outside the law (though I am not free from God's law but am under Christ's law) so that I might win those outside the law. To the weak I became weak, so that I might win the weak. I have become all things to all people, so that I might by any means save some. I do it all for the sake of the gospel, so that I may share in its blessings.

1 CORINTHIANS 9:16–23

Meditation: What does it mean for me "to be a slave to all" in the preaching of and witnessing to the Gospel? How do I become weak for the weak? Strong for the strong? Lost for the lost? Do I offer the Gospel "free of charge"? That is, do I offer the message of God's infinite mercy without any expectation of anything in return, including good results, praise for my efforts, material gain, self-satisfaction? How do I acquire a share of the Gospel by witnessing to it?

Pray: Lord God, you send us out as Apostles to spread the fruitful seed of your mercy. You provide us with all that we need to live your Word, to be your love, to draw others to your family. Make me an eager preacher of your Gospel, an able witness to your Good News in Christ. As Christ himself became all for all, make me a slave to all, so that I may follow behind him, being weak for the weak, strong for the strong. Let me draw no reward for this witness except a share in your Gospel. Amen.

DAY EIGHT: PRAYER IS A GRACE

Opening Prayer

[I]t is instructive to note the reaction of [a] Dominican of the sixteenth century, the down-to-earth Thomist, Francisco de Vitoria, to this sort of abstract mysticism. Vitoria writes: "There is a new kind of contemplation, which is practiced by the monks these days, consisting of meditating on God and the angels. They spend a long time in a state of elevation, thinking nothing. This is, no doubt, very good, but I do not find much about it in scripture, and it is, honestly, not what the saints recommend. Genuine contemplation is reading the bible and the study of true wisdom."

....[P]rayer or contemplation is not something that can be

achieved by mere human effort, however well-intentioned or however strenuous. Prayer is a grace. It is a gift that lifts us beyond anything we ourselves could ever attain by ascetic practice or by meditative technique. Accordingly, communion with God, actual friendship with God in prayer, although impossible even for the strong, is something God himself can achieve for us in a second, if he wishes. "Sometimes," a thirteenth century Dominican homily makes bold to declare, "a man is in a state of damnation before he begins his prayer, and before he is finished he is in a state of salvation!"

"RECOVERING THE CONTEMPLATIVE DIMENSION," 2001

Meditation: Meditating on my prayer life, what is it that I think I am doing when I pray? What behavior/attitude does the verb "to pray" describe? If prayer is a grace, then how do I understand my urge to pray as a gift? For a gift to be truly a gift, it must be received by the recipient with gratitude: in what way do I receive the grace of prayer as a gift? How do I express my gratitude once I have received this gift? What role does Scripture and the study of wisdom play in forming my prayer life? Do I see my prayer life as merely my work done for God, or do I see prayer as God's work done through me?

Pray: Lord God, you are the friend of all those who seek your wisdom and guidance. Though your Holy Spirit you prompt us to search and find that small still voice of love that shouts your name. With gratitude, I receive your gift of prayer. Give me the stamina I need to pray diligently and ask only for those graces that lead me closer to you. Keep me close to your Word in Scripture, and open my heart and mind to the study of your wisdom. Amen.

DAY NINE: THE LEAST OF THE LORD'S

Opening Prayer

"When the Son of Man comes in his glory, and all the angels with him, then he will sit on the throne of his glory. All the nations will be gathered before him, and he will separate people one from another as a shepherd separates the sheep from the goats, and he will put the sheep at his right hand and the goats at the left. Then the king will say to those at his right hand, 'Come, you that are blessed by my Father, inherit the kingdom prepared for you from the foundation of the world; for I was hungry and you gave me food, I was thirsty and you gave me something to drink, I was a stranger and you welcomed me, 36I was naked and you gave me clothing, I was sick and you took care of me, I was in prison and you visited me.' Then the righteous will answer him, 'Lord, when was it that we saw you hungry and gave you food, or thirsty and gave you something to drink? And when was it that we saw you a stranger and welcomed you, or naked and gave you clothing? And when was it that we saw you sick or in prison and visited you?' And the king will answer them, 'Truly I tell you, just as you did it to one of the least of these who are members of my family, you did it to me.'"

MATTHEW 25:31–40

Meditation: If it is true that we love God most when we love and serve the least of his, how do I love God? Quite literally, what do I do to love God? If righteous is based on establishing a "right relationship" with God through Christ, how do I cooperate with the graces I have been given in order to right my relationship with God? What does it mean to me to be an heir to the kingdom? How do I share the wealth of this kingdom? What impedes me from showing the generosity, care, and stewardship of the kingdom's abundant treasury of graces? Concretely, how do I live day-to-day "in the kingdom" while waiting on "the kingdom to come"?

Pray: King of kings, in our pursuit of holiness, we long for your righteousness. You have given us all that we need to see and hear the Gospel spoken and done. Help me to right my relationship with you through Christ Jesus. Show me those in most need and lead me to their care. Show me those most desperate for your mercy and make me an instrument of your compassion. With the least of yours among us, we cannot rest. Amen.

Novena to the Sacred Heart of Jesus

For Christians, the heart is the seat of the new covenant, the center of our new being, and the tabernacle of Christ's presence in us. Into our hearts, Christ pours his wisdom, his beauty, and his love. This Novena of the Sacred Heart trains our hearts and minds to receive in gratitude all of the gifts our Lord will give us.

Pray before a crucifix or a statue of the Sacred Heart.

Jesus Divine, you say to us, "Ask and you shall receive; seek and you shall find; knock and it shall be opened to you." Here I am, Lord, kneeling at your feet. Though I am in need, my heart is strong when I trust in you. My mind is sharp when turned to your Word. I have complete confidence in the promises your Sacred Heart made to Saint Margaret Mary. I come to you to give you thanks and praise and to ask for your help.

First, give thanks and praise;
ask for the specific help you need.

Lord, if I cannot turn to you for help, there is no one to help me. Your Sacred Heart is the source of all wisdom, all grace, all saving merit. Where could I look if not in the treasury that holds for us every blessing of your kindness and mercy? Lord, from the treasury of your Sacred Heart, please help me.

Lord, if I cannot knock at the door through which God gives himself to us, I cannot enter and go to him when he calls. By your mercy, I have recourse to you, Heart of Jesus, the door to the Father. In you, I find comfort when anxious, protection when in danger, strength when overburdened, and light in doubting darkness.

Jesus Divine, I know with heart and mind turned to your Word, that you will give me every gift I need to grow in your way. I receive now every gift you have given me, every gift you will ever give me, and I receive them all in gratitude and with praise for your name.

Lord, my heart is empty when I neglect your love and fail to love my neighbor as you have commanded. I know that without you I am not worthy of your gifts. But this is no reason for me to be discouraged. You, the eternal gift, are with me always! Gift and giver, you are the heart of mercy, the wellspring of all grace. You will not abandon a truly remorseful heart.

Therefore, Lord, look at me and see a servant in need. See my weaknesses, my failures. See, as well, my heart emptied of all disobedience, rebellion, every wrongdoing, and fill me with the eternal success of your sacrifice, your once-for-all offering on the cross. Seat yourself on the throne of my heart. Shine out your beauty through my words and deeds. Make me a lover of all your creatures. And bring me to your right hand in heaven.

Sacred Heart of Jesus, I adore you now and always; I love you now and always; I praise you now and always; and I will serve you to my dying day. My Jesus, accept my perfect surrender to your will for me. Give me every gift I need to live faithfully in your way, your truth, and your life. Amen.

Offering

My Father in heaven, I unite all my prayers, words, and deeds, my joys and sufferings, to the Sacred Heart of Jesus. I offer them to you in sacrifice as he offers himself in the holy sacrifice of the Mass. With thanksgiving, I offer to your service my body and soul, heart and mind, hands and feet. With Christ on the cross, I promise now to do as he did and work tirelessly for the earthly and eternal welfare of myself and my neighbors; for the needs of our holy Mother the Church; for the conversion of all your people; and for the relief of the poor here among us and those in purgatory.

Novena for Detachment and Holy Obedience

In his 1994 letter to the Order of Preachers, "Vowed to Mission," Father Timothy Radcliffe, OP, notes that in our deeply consumerist culture "the vow of Obedience goes against an understanding of being human as rooted in radical autonomy and individualism...." Often understood as mere compliance with authority, and therefore contrary to individual autonomy, obedience is thought to be oppressive and damaging to the freedom we ought to enjoy as citizens of the world. Christians, however, are committed by their baptismal vows to a freedom that transcends simple civil liberty. The perfect freedom won for us by Christ is freedom from sin so that we might be free to do his Father's will. First, obedience frees us to listen to what the Holy Spirit has to say to us. Then we are free to comply with the Father's will. The thirteenth-century German Dominican friar, Meister Eckhart, teaches that we will only grow in holiness if we bind together obedience and detachment—obedience to God's will and detachment from all things, especially one's self-centered will. Only by emptying ourselves of self can we be truly filled by God with God. The daily readings for this novena are taken from his conference, "Counsels on Discernment," quoted in *Meister Eckhart: The Essential Sermons, Commentaries, Treatises, and Defense.*

Daily Opening Prayer

Lord, Spirit of compassion, we seek the best of everything when we seek you alone. Though we are often held captive by our attachments in this world, we strive with all your graces to live in the freedom Christ won for us. Help me to root out everything that keeps me tied to my selfish will and to worldly distractions. My will is perfected in yours. Holding nothing back, I turn everything I have and everything I am over to you. Amen.

DAY ONE

True and perfect obedience is a virtue above all virtues, and no work is so great that it can be achieved or done without this virtue; and however little and however humble a work may be, it is done to greater profit in true obedience...take as humble a work as you like, whatever it may be, true obedience makes it finer and better for you (247).

DAY TWO

Obedience always produces the best of everything in everything. Truly, obedience never perturbs, never fails, whatever one is doing, in anything that comes from true obedience, for obedience neglects nothing that is good. Obedience need never be troubled, for it lacks no good thing (247).

DAY THREE

When a man in obedience goes out of himself and renounces what he possesses, God must necessarily respond by going in there, for if anyone does not want something for himself, God must want it as if for himself... So in all things, when I do not want something for myself, God wants it for me (247–8).

DAY FOUR

Now pay good heed. What is it that God wants for me that I do not want for myself? When I empty myself of self, he must necessarily want everything for me that he wants for himself, neither more nor less, and in the same manner he wants it for himself. And if he were not to do this, by that truth which is God, he would not be just, nor would he be the God that it is his nature to be (248).

DAY FIVE

In true obedience there should be no trace of "I want it so, and so," or "I want this or that," but there should be a pure going out from what is yours. And therefore in the best of all prayers that a man can pray, there should not be "Give me this virtue or that way of life," or "Yes, Lord, give me yourself, or give me everlasting life," but "Lord, give me nothing but what you will, and do, Lord, whatever and however you will in every way" (248).

DAY SIX

An empty spirit is one that is confused by nothing, attached to nothing, has not attached its best to any fixed way of acting, and has no concern whatever in anything for its own gain, for it is all sunk deep down into God's dearest will and has forsaken it own. A man can never perform any work, however humble, without it gaining strength and power from this (248–9).

DAY SEVEN

We can think what we like, that a man ought to shun one thing and pursue another—places and people and ways of life and environments and undertakings—that is not the trouble, such ways of life or such matters are not what impedes you. It is what you are in these things that causes the trouble, because in them you do not govern yourself as you should (249).

DAY EIGHT

Therefore, make a start with yourself, and abandon yourself. Truly, of you do not begin getting away from yourself, wherever you run to, you will find obstacles and trouble wherever it may be. People who seek peace in external things—be it in places or ways of life or people or activities or solitude or poverty or degradation however great such a thing may be or whatever it may be, still it is all nothing and gives no peace (249).

DAY NINE

The man who has God essentially present to him grasps God divinely, and to him God shines in all things; for everything tastes to him of God, and God forms himself for the man out of all things. God always shines out in him, in him there is a detachment and a turning away, and a forming of his God whom he loves and who is present to him. It is like a man consumed with a real and burning thirst, who may well not drink and may turn his mind to other things. But whatever he may do...the idea of drinking does not leave him, so long as he is thirsty (253).

Daily Meditation

Eckhart asks us to consider this question: What do I want for myself that God does not want for me? This is an extraordinarily difficult question to answer if we are not living in the Father's will for us. How often do we mistake "what I want" for "what God wants for me"? Without miraculous intervention, we may think knowing God's will for us is improbable, if not impossible. However, putting aside—detaching from all the possessive distractions that lay claim to your energy and attention and then listening to His Spirit—is a first good step toward finding a "desert" in your soul where the Word can be heard clearly and correctly. What has a claim on you? Who has such a claim? How do you treat these claims? Do they own you, possess you? To whom do you listen? With whom do you comply? Eckhart is not calling you away from compassion and responsibility. He is teaching us that we must understand these claims in terms of our Lord's singular and primary claim on our energy and attention. For the Christian who strives to grow in holiness, all such claims, all such attachments will find their ultimate meaning and worth only when understood as growing out of his love for us. By laying aside all worldly attachments, we place them in their proper order behind and below the principal attachment that renders all others possible: God's love for us!

Novena for Discernment of a Priestly Vocation

In the Name of the Father (+) and of the Son and of the Holy Spirit. Amen.

Daily Opening Prayer

Blessed Trinity, Merciful God, I come before you to ask for your help. You have moved my spirit and prompted me to consider giving my life to the service of your Church as a priest. Though I am obedient, there are many questions, doubts, and temptations that must be overcome before I am able to give myself freely to this call. I ask you to help me see your will for me; to hear your Word spoken to me; and to feel the fire of your Spirit setting me free to follow my gifts to perfect happiness in service to you. I ask all this in Jesus' holy name. Amen.

FIRST DAY

Daily Opening Prayer

Then Jesus went about all the cities and villages, teaching in their synagogues, and proclaiming the good news of the kingdom, and curing every disease and every sickness. When he saw the crowds, he had compassion for them, because they were harassed and helpless, like sheep without a shepherd. Then he said to his disciples, "The harvest is plentiful, but the labourers are few; therefore ask the Lord of the harvest to send out labourers into his harvest."

MATTHEW 9:35–38

Meditation: What is it precisely that makes me think I have a priestly vocation?

Challenge: To be ordered to Christ the Head of the Church is to be ordered in servant-leadership for the whole Body. Can you see your vocation to the priesthood as a gift of humble service to the Church?

Act of Humility: O divine Lord, I approach you in wonder and awe, knowing that I have not always surrendered myself to your will. On my own, I am not worthy to have you enter my home; but only speak the word and my soul will be healed. With humility, I ask you to clarify in my heart and mind the call to service you have given me. In the same way that our Blessed Mother said yes to your call to bring the Word into the world, I too desire nothing more than to be a preacher and prophet of your grace. Help me, Lord, to see clearly! Amen.

SECOND DAY

Daily Opening Prayer

Then someone came to him and said, "Teacher, what good deed must I do to have eternal life?" And he said to him, "Why do you ask me about what is good? There is only one who is good. If you wish to enter into life, keep the commandments." He said to him, "Which ones?" And Jesus said, "You shall not murder; You shall not commit adultery; You shall not steal; You shall not bear false witness; Honour your father and mother; also, You shall love your neighbour as yourself." The young man said to him, "I have kept all these; what do I still lack?" Jesus said to him, "If you wish to be perfect, go, sell your possessions, and give the money to the poor, and you will have treasure in heaven; then come, follow me." When the young man heard this word, he went away grieving, for he had many possessions.

Then Jesus said to his disciples, "Truly I tell you, it will be hard for a rich person to enter the kingdom of heaven. Again I tell you, it is easier for a camel to go through the eye of a needle than for someone who is rich to enter the kingdom of God." When the disciples heard this, they were greatly astounded and said, "Then who can be saved?" But Jesus looked at them and said, "For mortals it is impossible, but for God all things are possible."

Then Peter said in reply, "Look, we have left everything and followed you. What then will we have?" Jesus said to them, "Truly I tell you, at the renewal of all things, when the Son of Man is seated on the throne of his glory, you who have followed me will also sit on twelve thrones, judging the twelve tribes of Israel. And everyone who has left houses or brothers or sisters or father or mother or children or fields, for my name's sake, will receive a hundredfold, and will inherit eternal life. But many who are first will be last, and the last will be first."

MATTHEW 19:16–30

Meditation: What gifts do I have that can be perfected in the service of the Church as a priest?

Challenge: God's grace, his gifts to you, build on our nature, providing you with abundant means for perfecting his love in you by serving others. Can you see your gifts as graced means of revealing God's love to others?

Act of Generosity: O divine Lord, I approach you in wonder and awe, knowing that I have not always used the gifts you have given me in the service of others. I know that you perfect your love in those who love you and neighbor first, so I ask that you show me my gifts, the graces you have given me for my perfection, that I might generously share your abundant love with all those who will see your face in mine and hear your Word when I speak. Help me to be openhanded with all I have, especially the gift of my life in your service. Amen.

THIRD DAY

Daily Opening Prayer
He went up the mountain and called to him those whom he wanted, and they came to him.

MARK 3:13

Meditation: Am I willing to surrender my plans for my life and pledge obedience to my bishop or religious superior?

Challenge: Serving others in the Church means giving up any plans you might have for your life. Priesthood is a form of kenosis, a self-emptying that imitates Christ in his Incarnation and on the cross. Can you see your vocation as a call to pour out your plans, your expectations, your dreams, and to take up the cross of service?

Act of Sacrifice: O divine Lord, I approach you in wonder and awe, knowing that I have not always used the gifts you have given me in the service of others. I know you call those whom you want to lead lives of selfless sacrifice. As I discern your call, show me the way of self-emptying that I may be better prepared to be filled with the gifts I will need to teach and preach your Gospel. In all things, I hope to follow you, even to the cross. Amen.

FOURTH DAY

Daily Opening Prayer

Now large crowds were travelling with him; and he turned and said to them, "Whoever comes to me and does not hate father and mother, wife and children, brothers and sisters, yes, and even life itself, cannot be my disciple. Whoever does not carry the cross and follow me cannot be my disciple. For which of you, intending to build a tower, does not first sit down and estimate the cost, to see whether he has enough to complete it? Otherwise, when he has laid a foundation and is not able to finish, all who see it will begin to ridicule him, saying, 'This fellow began to build and was not able to finish.' Or what king, going out to wage war against another king, will not sit down first and consider whether he is able with ten thousand to oppose the one who comes against him with twenty thousand? If he cannot, then, while the other is still far away, he sends a delegation and asks for the terms of peace. So therefore, none of you can become my disciple if you do not give up all your possessions."

LUKE 14:25–33

Meditation: Strength comes with exercise. What cross do I carry now? What burden do I carry in Christ's name for his sake?

Challenge: "Carrying a cross" is our Lord's way of challenging us to consider what it is we are willing to die for. As a priest, you will be called upon to "die" many times in your life of service. Can you carry your cross with patience, determination, perseverance, and love? Can you resist the temptations that will lure you to ease the burden of your priestly ministry—vanity, power, luxury, disobedience, prestige, ridicule?

Act of Submission: O divine Lord, I approach you in wonder and awe, knowing that I have not always used the gifts you have given me in the service of others. Though I am weak, I desire to be strong in you. Though I am reluctant to suffer, I long to consecrate the burdens I carry to your service in the Church. I freely submit what strength I have to your ministry of mercy. Help me to exercise that strength so I may continue to follow on your way, carrying my cross behind you. Amen.

FIFTH DAY

Daily Opening Prayer

I appeal to you therefore, brothers and sisters, by the mercies of God, to present your bodies as a living sacrifice, holy and acceptable to God, which is your spiritual worship. Do not be conformed to this world, but be transformed by the renewing of your minds, so that you may discern what is the will of God—what is good and acceptable and perfect.

ROMANS 12:1–2

Meditation: How have I conformed myself to this present age? How am I an example of my culture right now?

Challenge: We are all called to be in the world but not of it. Our mission of Gospel proclamation often sets us against the expectations and demands of our culture. Each of us carries the marks of our upbringing in our attitudes, values, and habits. Paul urges us not to be conformed to this age "so that we might discern." How are the marks of your conformation to this age preventing you from discerning God's will for you?

Act of Conformity to Christ: O divine Lord, I approach you in wonder and awe, knowing that I have not always used the gifts you have given me in the service of others. Having conformed myself in many ways to this present age, I long to be conformed to you alone. That I might better discern your will for me, show me the light of your sacrificial love, remake me in your image. Recreate me with a clean heart, a holy mind, and a body eager for spiritual worship. Amen.

SIXTH DAY

Daily Opening Prayer

Live by the Spirit, I say, and do not gratify the desires of the flesh. For what the flesh desires is opposed to the Spirit, and what the Spirit desires is opposed to the flesh; for these are opposed to each other, to prevent you from doing what you want. But if you are led by the Spirit, you are not subject to the law. Now the works of the flesh are obvious: fornication, impurity, licentiousness, idolatry, sorcery, enmities, strife, jealousy, anger, quarrels, dissensions, factions, envy, drunkenness, carousing, and things like these. I am warning you, as I warned you before: those who do such things will not inherit the kingdom of God.

By contrast, the fruit of the Spirit is love, joy, peace, patience, kindness, generosity, faithfulness, gentleness, and self-control. There is no law against such things. And those who belong to Christ Jesus have crucified the flesh with its passions and desires. If we live by the Spirit, let us also be guided by the Spirit. Let us not become conceited, competing against one another, envying one another.

GALATIANS 5:16–26

Meditation: How do I "live by the Spirit"? What do I do that I do not want to do?

Challenge: To live by the Spirit is not a call to live an angelic life in the flesh. Rather, as children of the Spirit, we have promised to work against "the desires of our sinful natures" and produce the good fruits of the Spirit to whom we belong. This means that we lift up and nurture the goodness of our creation rather than wallowing in our falleness. As a priest you will serve as an example to those you lead and serve. How are you tempted to work against producing the good fruits of the Spirit in you?

Act of Holiness: O divine Lord, I approach you in wonder and awe, knowing that I have not always used the gifts you have given me in the service of others. I know from your unfailing Word that the good fruits of the Spirit are love, joy, peace, patience, kindness, goodness, faithfulness, gentleness, and self-control. I know as well that I often fail to produce these good fruits by indulging the desires of my sinful nature. Help me to lift up and nurture the goodness of my creation by living a life of holiness in your Spirit. Amen.

SEVENTH DAY

Daily Opening Prayer
I have heard of your faith in the Lord Jesus and your love towards all the saints, and for this reason I do not cease to give thanks for you as I remember you in my prayers. I pray that the God of our Lord Jesus Christ, the Father of glory, may give you a spirit of wisdom and revelation as you come to know him, so that, with the eyes of your heart enlightened, you may know what is the hope to which he has called you, what are the riches of his glorious inheritance among the saints, and what is the immeasurable greatness of his power for us who believe, according to the working of his great power. God put this power to work in Christ

when he raised him from the dead and seated him at his right hand in the heavenly places, far above all rule and authority and power and dominion, and above every name that is named, not only in this age but also in the age to come.

EPHESIANS 1:15–21

Meditation: What do you hope for? Where do you place your hope—in the things of this world (money, politics, prestige), your personal development, God?

Challenge: In his letter to the Ephesians, Paul prays that "the Father of glory, may give you a spirit of wisdom and revelation resulting in knowledge of him." As a man discerning a vocation to the priesthood, a spirit of wisdom and revelation is vital to your listening. Hope is not a form of gambling but rather a kind of knowledge, a knowing, a certainty that God's promises have already been fulfilled in Christ. What more do you need from God to experience this enlightenment? What do you need to listen attentively?

Act of Enlightenment: O divine Lord, I approach you in wonder and awe, knowing that I have not always used the gifts you have given me in the service of others. You are a faithful God, steadfast in your promises and generous in your kindness. Look on my doubts, fears, and worldly expectations; transform them into the one hope that reveals your wisdom and the riches of your glory. Open the eyes of my heart so that I might see your will for me and lead among your holy ones. Amen.

EIGHTH DAY

Daily Opening Prayer

And every priest stands day after day at his service, offering again and again the same sacrifices that can never take away sins. But when Christ had offered for all time a single sacrifice for sins, "he sat down at the right hand of God," and since then has been waiting "until his enemies would be made a footstool for his feet." For by a single offering he has perfected for all time those who are sanctified. And the Holy Spirit also testifies to us, for after saying,

"This is the covenant that I will make with them
after those days, says the Lord:
I will put my laws in their hearts,
and I will write them on their minds,"
he also adds,
"I will remember their sins and their lawless deeds no more."

HEBREWS 10:11–17

Meditation: Am I prepared to stand daily in a priestly ministry of sacrificial service to the Church? How do I understand the difference between "being a priest" and "functioning as a priest"?

Challenge: Christ offered one sacrifice for the forgiveness of our sins. As a priest, you will offer this same sacrifice in the Eucharist, leading God's people in the Paschal Feast that draws them ever closer to their Lord. Being a priest is a daily, hourly, minute-by-minute existence; it is not a function or a job, but a way of being for the Church. In Hebrews, we read the Lord saying, "I will put my laws in their hearts, and I will write them upon their minds." This is not a job description for an employee but a radical renewal of your existence. Are you open to this transformation, to be one who offers the sacraments of the Church as way of being Christ for others?

Act of Consecration: O divine Lord, I approach you in wonder and awe, knowing that I have not always used the gifts you have given me in the service of others. I read in your Word that "we have been consecrated through the offering of the body of Jesus Christ once for all." I know that in my baptism I have been consecrated to your service and share in your ministry to the world. Is it your will for me that I should stand daily at the altar of your Body and offer the sacraments of salvation to your people? Speak to me so that I may hear. Open my heart that I may listen. Amen.

NINTH DAY

Daily Opening Prayer

We know that the whole creation has been groaning in labour pains until now; and not only the creation, but we ourselves, who have the first fruits of the Spirit, groan inwardly while we wait for adoption, the redemption of our bodies. For in hope we were saved. Now hope that is seen is not hope. For who hopes for what is seen? But if we hope for what we do not see, we wait for it with patience.

Likewise the Spirit helps us in our weakness; for we do not know how to pray as we ought, but that very Spirit intercedes with sighs too deep for words. And God, who searches the heart, knows what is the mind of the Spirit, because the Spirit intercedes for the saints according to the will of God.

We know that all things work together for good for those who love God, who are called according to his purpose.

ROMANS 8:22–28

Meditation: What is my purpose? For what end was I created? Do I think and speak and act as a man created in goodness by a good and faithful God?

Challenge: We are able to love because we are first loved by God. We were created in love and remain in being in virtue of his love for us. That we were created in love means that we were created for a purpose: to love in return and to return to love himself. In all you will do as a priest, you will point to and make present this divine love. Whether you are celebrating the Eucharist, counseling the despairing, or preparing a homily—everything you do will be a sign of divine love. Are you prepared for the challenge of being a living sign of the love that created the universe and re-created it in Christ?

Act of Love: O divine Lord, I approach you in wonder and awe, knowing that I have not always used the gifts you have given me in the service of others. I read in your Word "that the whole creation has been groaning in labour pains until now" (Romans 8:22), waiting for our redemption. Though I do not always live a life of love for you and others, I know that my created purpose is to be your love for my neighbor. Even as I discern your will for me, your Spirit groans within me, pushing me to love more and better. Where it is your will for me, I know it will be for the good. Amen.

Part Two
The Litanies

Litany of God the Father

Lord, have mercy on us. **Lord, have mercy on us.**
Christ, have mercy on us. **Christ, have mercy on us.**
Lord, have mercy on us. **Lord, have mercy on us.**

God the Father, Maker of heaven and earth,
Hear our prayer.
God the Son, Savior of all creation,
God the Holy Spirit, Divine Love among us.

Holy Trinity, One God,
Have mercy on us.
Holy Trinity, Three Persons,
Holy Trinity, One God.

The Father, First Person of the Blessed Trinity,
Hear us and bless us.
The only Son, Second Person and Messiah,
The Holy Spirit, Third Person and Divine Love proceeding,
Father of the Blessed Virgin, conceived without sin,
Father of Joseph, her faithful spouse.

Our Father in heaven,
Blessed is your name.
Father, eternal being,
Father, infinite glory,
Father, infinite beauty,
Father, infinite goodness,
Father, infinite joy,
Father, infinite power,

Father, infinite wisdom,
Father, infinite justice,
Father, infinite mercy,
Father, infinite truth,
Father, infinite presence.

Father, creator of Heaven and earth,
Your kingdom comes.
Father, you hold all creation in being,
Father, you are our final end,
Father, you promised a Savior,
Father, you are revealed by the Son,
Father, you will the passion of Jesus,
Father, you accept the Sacrifice of Calvary,
Father, you reconcile with mankind,
Father, you send the Holy Spirit,
Father, in the Name of Christ Jesus.

Father of all Nations and Peoples, **Your will be done.**
Father of the poor and oppressed,
Father of the homeless and hungry
Father of widows and widowers,
Father of the exiled and outcast,
Father of the persecuted and the bullied,
Father of the troubled and disturbed,
Father of the sick and injured,
Father of the unborn and the aged.

Father, you are Love,   **Treasure us.**
Father, you are Holiness,   **Bless us.**
Father, you are Wisdom,   **Enlighten us.**

Father, you are Providence,	**Care for us.**
Father, we adore you.	**We adore you.**
Father, we love you.	**We love you.**
Father, we thank you.	**We thank you.**
Father, we bless you.	**We bless you.**

| In good times and bad, | **Let us bless you.** |

In disease and in wellness,
In blessing and when tempted,
In comfort and in despair,
In celebration and in mourning,
In joy and in anguish,
In life and in death,
In time and through eternity.

Father, hear us.

Father, graciously hear us.

Lamb of God, beloved Son of the Father,

Spare us, O Lord.

Lamb of God, who commanded perfection

Graciously hear us, O Lord.

Lamb of God, only Mediator with the Father,

Have mercy on us.

Let us pray: Our Father…

Closing Prayer

Father, you give us all that we need to come to you perfected as Christ himself is perfect. We honor you and worship you as our Creator, our Lord, and as our only Father in heaven. Hear us as we offer these praises, lifted up as incense before your throne, and grant us all we need to be your faithful children, loving brothers and sisters to Christ Jesus. In his name we pray. Amen.

Litany of Jesus, Priest and Sacrifice

Lord, have mercy on us. **He is mercy forever.**
Christ, have mercy on us. **He is compassion forever.**
Lord, have mercy on us. **He is mercy forever.**

Christ, hear us. **Christ, graciously hear us.**
Lord, hear us. **Lord, graciously hear us.**
Christ, hear us. **Christ, graciously hear us.**

God the Father, who spoke the Word
You are mercy forever.
God the Son, who is Word spoken,
God the Holy Spirit, the breath of the Word.

Holy Trinity, one God, **You are love forever.**
Three Persons, one God,
Holy Trinity, one God,

Jesus, you are Priest and Sacrifice,
Lamb of God, you died for us.
Jesus, you are Sacrifice and Altar,
Jesus, Priest in the order of Melchizedek,
Jesus, Priest sent to preach the Father's mercy,
Jesus, Priest of the Sacrifice of the Mass,
Jesus, Priest, a living intercession for us.

Jesus, High Priest taken from among the men of the tribes,
We thank you, Lord!
Jesus, High Priest appointed for the sake of all mankind,
Jesus, High Priest anointed by the Father with the Holy Spirit,

Jesus, High Priest of a greater dignity than Moses,
Jesus, High Priest, guiltless and clean,
Jesus, High Priest, faithful and merciful,
Jesus, High Priest, fully human, perfect forever,
Jesus, High Priest, fully divine, perfect forever,
Jesus, High Priest of our love and trust,
Jesus, High Priest of God, zealous for our souls,
Jesus, High Priest of our heart's true tabernacle,
Jesus, High Priest of our final end and life eternal,
Jesus, High Priest, who enters the heavenly temple,
Jesus, High Priest, who offers yourself as a sacrifice to God,
Jesus, High Priest, who washes us clean from sin,
Jesus, High Priest, who gives us eternal life.

Jesus, sacrifice to God for all men,
Blessed be the Lamb forever!
Jesus, holy and immaculate sacrifice,
Jesus, reconciling sacrifice,
Jesus, peace-bringing sacrifice,
Jesus, our Sacrifice of praise and thanksgiving,
Jesus, our Sacrifice of reunion and serenity,
Jesus, our Sacrifice through whom we have sure access to God,
Jesus, our Sacrifice for life eternal.

Be merciful!	**Spare us, O Jesus.**
Be merciful!	**Graciously hear us, O Jesus.**
Be merciful!	**Spare us, O Jesus.**

You were ordained Priest by God the Father,
You deliver us, O Jesus.
Through your eternal priesthood,
Through your holy anointing,
Through your priestly spirit,
Through your ministry you glorify the Father,
Through your one sacrifice upon the cross,
Through your Sacrifice remembered upon the altar,
Through your Divine power,
Through your human suffering,
Through your royal priests, the baptized,
Through your ministerial priests, the ordained.

Grant peace to your ordained ministers.
We beg you, O Lord.
Preserve all your priests in holiness of life.
Fill them with the spirit of priestly service.
Grant that their lips may speak the Truth.
Grant that their hands may do your Work.
Grant that their feet may walk in your Way.
Grant that their hearts may be tabernacles of your Presence.
Grant that their minds may be formed in holy knowledge.
Grant to them endurance in your service.
Grant to them humility and wisdom in ministry.
Grant to them skill in action and fidelity in prayer.
Send diligent and faithful workers into your harvest.
Send faithful men to be stewards of your Church's mysteries.
Promote through them the adoration of the Blessed Sacrament.
Receive into your joy all those who have served you faithfully.

O, Lamb of God, you take away the sins of the world,
Spare us, O Lord.
O, Lamb of God, you take away the sins of the world,
Graciously hear us, O Lord.
Lamb of God, you take away the sins of the world,
Have mercy on us, O Lord.

Let us pray: O Jesus, our Sacrifice and High Priest, you bless and guard your Church. Through your Holy Spirit raise up within the Body men worthy to be faithful servants of your people through the Church's sacraments. By their ministry and example will your Christian people be instructed in the truth of the faith and led to holiness along your way. Grant to all the baptized, O Lord, the gifts they need to be better priests, better sacrifices for the salvation of all the world. We ask this through Christ, our priest and our altar. Amen.

Litany of the Most Holy Trinity

Blessed be the Holy Trinity, indivisible Unity;
Glory to Him for His mercy!
O Lord, how wonderful is your Name in all the earth!
How deep the riches of His wisdom and knowledge!

God the Father of heaven and earth,
You are mercy forever.
God the Son, Redeemer of the world,
God the Holy Ghost, fire of the Church,
Holy Trinity, Three Persons, One God.

Father from Whom all things are,
Son through Whom all things are,
Holy Ghost in Whom all things are,
Holy and undivided Trinity,
Father infinite and everlasting, Only-begotten Son of the Father,
Spirit who precedes from the Father and the Son,
Co-eternal Majesty of Three Divine Persons,
Father, Creator,
Son, Redeemer,
Holy Spirit, Advocate,
Holy, holy, holy Lord, God of angels and saints.

Who was, Who is, Who will be,
Who came, Who comes, Who will come,
Who loved, Who loves, Who will love,
Lord Most High, Who dwells eternally,
Who alone is worthy of honor and glory,
Who alone does great wonders,

Power infinite, eternal presence,
Incomprehensible Wisdom,
Unsayable Love, Architect of creation,

From all dark angels, **Deliver us, O Holy Trinity.**
From all disobedience,
From all arrogance,
From all love of riches,
From all impurities,
From all refusal of joy,
From all disordered affections,
From all jealousy and cruelty,
From all anger and impatience,
From every thought, word, and deed contrary to charity,
From the unpardonable sin,
Through your plentiful loving-kindness,
Through your treasure of goodness and love,
Through your wisdom and knowledge,
Through all your unsayable perfections.

We redeemed sinners ask you, Lord, **Hear us!**
That we may always serve you alone,
That we may worship you in spirit and in truth,
That we may love you with all our heart,
That we may love you with all our soul,
That we may love you with all our strength,
That we may love our neighbor as ourselves,
That we may keep your holy commandments,
That we may never pollute our bodies and souls with sin,
That we may go from grace to grace, and from virtue to virtue,
That we may finally enjoy your beauty.

O Blessed Trinity,	**Deliver us.**
O Blessed Trinity,	**Save us.**
O Blessed Trinity,	**Forgive us.**

Let us pray: Our Father…

V. Blessed are you, O Lord, on the Throne of Heaven,
R. You are worthy of praise and exhalation forever.

Let us pray: Eternal God, in this profession of the true faith you have gifted your servants with the grace needed to know and love the glory of your eternal Trinity. In the power of your majesty, we come to adore the holy unity of three divine Persons in one God. We beg you for the strength and wisdom of the apostolic faith that we may come to know and love the community of persons within your Church and live the divine life to your perfection in heaven. We ask this through Jesus Christ, our Lord. Amen.

Litany to the Infant Jesus

Father, Son, and Holy Spirit, **Hear us and have mercy.**

Creator, Redeemer, and Advocate, Father of us all, we come to you as your children, confident that all we need to grow in holiness is your gift. You give us every good thing; you created us, you re-created us, and you hold us in being. As you came among us as a child from the Virgin's womb, fully human and fully divine, we pray that we may return to you with the faith of a child, perfectly human, whole and holy. We pray this litany so that we may come to know and love the perfect trust of the infant Jesus. Hear us, Lord, as we pray:

Infant Jesus, the Christ, Emmauel,
>**Give us a child's faith.**
Infant Jesus, True God, our only Savior,
Infant Jesus, only Son of the living God,
Infant Jesus, Son of the blessed Virgin Mary,
Infant Jesus, Strength in weakness,
Infant Jesus, Power in compassion, Infant Jesus, Wealth of graces,
Infant Jesus, Well-spring of love,
Infant Jesus, Renewal of the heavens,
Infant Jesus, Repair for creation's evils,
Infant Jesus, Prince of angels,
Infant Jesus, Root of the patriarchs,
Infant Jesus, Word of the prophets,
Infant Jesus, Desire of the nations,
Infant Jesus, Joy of shepherds,
Infant Jesus, Star of the Magi,

Infant Jesus, Redemption of infants,
Infant Jesus, Hope of the just,
Infant Jesus, Teacher of the wise,
Infant Jesus, First-fruit of the dead.

Be merciful and hear us,   **O Infant Jesus.**
Be merciful and give us a child's faith.

From the slavery of Adam's rebellion,

Deliver us, Infant Jesus.

From slavery to the devil,
From the longings of the flesh,
From the spite of the world,
From the serpent's temptation of pride,
From the disordered desire for knowledge,
From the blindness of a sinful spirit,
From the evil of abortion and contraception,
From our willful hearts and obstinate minds.

Through your sinless conception,
Through your humble birth,
Through your painful circumcision,
Through your wonderful epiphany,
Through your presentation in the temple,
Through your poverty, chastity, and obedience,
Through your missions and miracles,
Through your teaching and preaching,
Through your many sufferings and despair,
Through your death on the cross,
Through your burial and descent into hell,
Through your resurrection and ascension,

Through your divine life in the Blessed Trinity,
And from the right hand of the Father.

Lamb of God, you take away the sins of the world,
Have mercy on us, Infant Jesus.
Lamb of God, you take away the sins of the world,
Graciously hear us, Infant Jesus.
Lamb of God, you take away the sins of the world,
Have mercy on us, Infant Jesus.

Let us pray: O Infant Jesus, it pleased you to become human like one of us, to be born in human history and become a child of the Blessed Virgin. Give us sight to see the infinite wisdom in the faith of a child; to see that there is power in weakness and majesty in humility. While adoring your humanity on earth, may we come to contemplate your glories in heaven. With the Father and the Holy Spirit, you live and reign forever and ever. Amen.

Litany to Mary, Co-Redemptrix

Though not yet formally defined as a dogma of the Church, the teaching that Mary is Co-Redemptrix is clearly taught in Scripture, tradition, papal teaching, and orthodox theology. The title "Co-Redemptrix" simply means that the Church understands that Mary is "a woman who cooperates in the work of the Redeemer." In no way is this title suggesting that Mary is "another Redeemer" or in some way "equal to" Christ as the only Redeemer of mankind. Mary as Co-Redemptrix is our example of a perfected human response to Christ's call to hear the Gospel, to take up our cross, to preach his Good News, and thereby perfect in us our Father's love for us. It is only through our free cooperation with God's grace that we are redeemed. In this way, we are all "co-redeemers" with Christ.

Opening Prayer

Presider: At the invitation of the archangel, Gabriel, the virgin Mary assented to give herself to the Holy Spirit, body and soul, to become the Mother of God. By surrendering herself to God's will, she gave his Word flesh and bone. By her consent, Mary became a worker with God in giving the gift of Christ to the world. She is the Mediatrix of All Graces, the Mother of the Church, and by suffering with Christ beneath the cross, she is her son's Co-Redemptrix, a woman with Christ in his redeeming work.

We pray this litany to honor her work with Christ in our redemption. We pray too that we may become faithful workers with Christ in our own salvation and the salvation of the whole world.

The Angelus

V. The angel spoke God's message to Mary

R. And she conceived of the Holy Spirit. Hail Mary, full of grace.

V. "I am the lowly servant of the Lord:

R. "Let it be done to me according to your word."

Hail Mary, full of grace…

V. And the Word became flesh

R. and lived among us. Hail Mary, full of grace…

V. Pray for us, holy Mother of God,

R. That we may become worthy of the promises of Christ.

Let us pray: Lord, fill our hearts with your grace: once, through the message of an angel you revealed to us the Incarnation of your Son; now, through his suffering and death lead us to the glory of his resurrection. We ask this through Christ our Lord. Amen.

The Litany

Mary, you said yes to Gabriel,

> **And the Holy Spirit came upon you;**

Mary, by the Holy Spirit,

> **You conceived in your womb the Christ Child;**

Mary, in your womb

> **You gifted our Savior with flesh and bone;**

Mary, pregnant with our Lord,

> **You visited Elizabeth and his herald, John;**

Mary, with Elizabeth and John

> **You rejoiced at the coming of our salvation.**

Recite the *Magnificat* (Mary's Song of Praise):

And Mary said,
'My soul magnifies the Lord,
*   and my spirit rejoices in God my Saviour,*
for he has looked with favour on the lowliness of his servant.
*   Surely, from now on all generations will call me blessed;*
for the Mighty One has done great things for me,
*   and holy is his name.*
His mercy is for those who fear him
*   from generation to generation.*
He has shown strength with his arm;
*   he has scattered the proud in the thoughts of their hearts.*
He has brought down the powerful from their thrones,
*   and lifted up the lowly;*
he has filled the hungry with good things,
*   and sent the rich away empty.*
He has helped his servant Israel,
*   in remembrance of his mercy,*
according to the promise he made to our ancestors,
*   to Abraham and to his descendants for ever.*

LUKE 1:46–55

Mary, in poorest Bethelem
You suffered the pains of childbirth;
Mary, among God's humble animals
You gave birth to Jesus;
Mary, with Joseph, your husband
You brought Christ into the world;
Mary, you accepted for Christ
The precious gifts of the Magi;
Mary, in Christ, your son
You gave us the Way, the Truth, and the Life.

Mary, mother and woman with Christ
You opened the bountiful Way;
Mary, mother and woman with Christ
You brought Truth to the world;
Mary, mother and woman with Christ
You gave life to Life eternal;
Mary, mother and woman with Christ
You worshiped at his feet;
Mary, mother and woman with Christ
You shed tears for his suffering.

Mary, disciple and preacher
You were his most faithful student;
Mary, disciple and preacher
You preached his Good News;
Mary, disciple and preacher
You took up your cross to follow him;
Mary, disciple and preacher
You made your body an acceptable sacrifice;
Mary, disciple and preacher
You followed him on his sorrowful way.

Mary, mother and woman with Christ
He wore a crown of thorns for your sake and ours;*
Mary, mother and woman with Christ
He was whipped for your sake and ours;
Mary, mother and woman with Christ
He carried his cross for your sake and ours;
Mary, mother and woman with Christ
He was nailed to the cross for your sake and ours.

Mary, mother and woman with Christ
> **He was forsaken to die for your sake and ours.**

Mary, Mother of the Lamb of God
> **Intercede for us at the altar of sacrifice;**

Mary, Mother of the Most Innocent Child
> **Intercede for us as our Advocate Mother;**

Mary, Mother of Christ Crucified
> **Intercede for us at the foot of the cross.**

Prayer to Mary, Co-Redemptrix

O Mary, Mother of God and Mother of his Church, you are the first preacher of the Word Made Flesh, Emmanuel, God-is-with-us. You consented to give our Savior flesh and blood, making him both human and divine, making him like one of us in all things but sin. You brought him into the world to save the world, and you were with him when he left this world to save it. Though Simeon prophesied that your son's suffering and death would pierce your heart, you did not surrender to sorrow or despair. Trusting in his promise of salvation, you lifted your cross as his mother; followed him on his way as his disciple; opened your heart to his truth as his preacher; and now, because of your perseverance, you live with him in eternal life as our advocate and his co-redemptrix.

Mary, Co-Redemptrix, you are a woman of unbounded faith and you teach us the beauty of trusting the Father. You are a woman of unbounded hope and you are all that we might hope to become in Christ. You are a woman of unbounded love, and so you are the mother of us all. We pray that as you contemplate the divine beauty of your resurrected son in heaven, you will remember your children in this world. Lift us up to the face of Christ, show him that you love us as you love him. And ask him to gift us with the grace we need to grow in our work toward holiness. Pray that we be given the strength and perseverance we need to become co-workers with Christ in our own redemption and the redemption of the whole world. In the name of Christ our Lord and with gratitude for the blessings we have been given, we receive those blessings as gifts and give Christ glory and praise. Amen.

---

*Mary was immaculately conceived in her mother's womb, born free from the burden of original sin. This immaculate conception, though preceding Christ's death and resurrection in history, was achieved from eternity as a singular grace in virtue of his sacrifice. In other words, Mary was a beneficiary of Christ's salvific death on the cross.

Litany to the Unsayable God

Saint Gregory of Nyssa writes in *On Virginity*, "Anyone who tries to describe the ineffable Light in language is truly a liar—not because he hates the truth, but because of the inadequacy of his description." Gregory of Nyssa is one of the Church's greatest voices for apophatic theology—"what God is not"—an approach to God that holds that we come to know God best by first understanding that we can never know God fully. This *via negativa* pushes us to acknowledge the woeful inadequacy of our theological language in mediating the truth of the Divine. What we are left with is an indirect experience of the Divine rooted in our invincible ignorance as finite creatures. However, prayer is our response to the Spirit's seduction, a seduction that draws us nearer to the Unapproachable. We pray not in order to perfect ourselves intellectually but rather to exhaust the imprecision of our words, images, logic, and science—an impossible task!—leaving us with a greater awareness of our ignorance and therefore an awareness of our greater need for God. In other words, we pray in humility in order to perfect God's love in us.

Opening Prayer

Lord, we know our words can never describe you. We know you are beyond description, beyond science, beyond logic and reason, beyond experience. And yet, you make yourself present to us in your creation, your Word, and in your Son, Christ Jesus. Your Holy Spirit moves us to pray this litany so that we might at once deepen our ignorance of your mystery and grow ever closer to your Divine Love in humility. In our darkness, Lord, show us your light. Amen.

The Litany

Our Lord dwells in light unapproachable.

In brilliant light He shines.

Our Lord is unspeakable brilliance.

The brilliance of every blazing star.

Our Lord is infinite ecstacy.

The ecstacy of all created things.

Our Lord is flawless Being.

The perfection of Being Himself.

Our Lord is all-knowing Presence.

He says, "I AM that I AM."

Our Lord is all-present Knowledge.

He knows every sparrow, every heart.

Our Lord is all-powerful Beauty.

He is harmony, serenity, and health.

Our Lord is all-beautiful Power.

For Him nothing is impossible.

He is unsayable.

Our Lord is inexhaustible Word.

He is ineffable.

Our Lord is beyond words, beyond reason.

He is without limits.

Our Lord is boundless Self.

He is incomparable.

Our Lord is exemplary Excellence.

He is unbroken.

Our Lord is One God, Three Persons.

He is pure.

Our Lord is Goodness itself.

He is immanent.

Our Lord is with us always.

He is transcendent.
>**Our Lord is wholly Other.**

He is the Way.
>**Our Lord is our Journey and Destination.**

He is Truth.
>**Our Lord is revealed Mystery.**

He is Life.
>**Our Lord is glory upon glory.**

He is God the Father.
>**Our Lord is creating Voice.**

He is God the Son.
>**Our Lord is re-creating Word.**

He is God the Holy Spirit.
>**Our Lord is the breath of Love.**

He is Perfection.
>**Our Lord is Being-beyond-Being.**

Let us pray: Unsayable God, we pray knowing our words are emptied of final meaning. We know that our prayer is the babble of infants in your ineffable presence; and yet, we are seduced by your divine love, the Holy Spirit, to send up our inarticulate groans, our meager words, so that we might deepen our ignorance and come to depend on you more and more for what wisdom we can harvest from your abundance. Wholly in love with you, we are true, good, and beautiful because we participate in you who are truth, goodness, and beauty. Hear us, Lord, in the name of your Incarnate Son, Christ Jesus. Amen.

Part Three

The Way-Truth-Life Rosary

Praying the Rosary

Long a means of growing closer to God through the intercession of the Blessed Virgin Mary, the rosary is the quintessential Catholic devotion. Praying the rosary is not only a way of offering thanks and praise to God, it is also a way of learning the core teachings of the Gospel preached by Jesus himself. The Way-Truth-Life Rosary devotion takes its start from the Gospel of John (15:5-6). "Thomas the disciple says to Jesus, 'Lord, we do not know where you are going. How can we know the way?' Jesus said to him, 'I am the way, and the truth, and the life. No one comes to the Father except through me. If you know me, you will know my Father also.'" The Christ comes to us as the Father promised: as the Word present at the moment of creation; the Word of Scripture; and the Word made flesh. Jesus is the way, the truth, and the life. This rosary devotion will lead you through Scripture to a better understanding of his self-revelation.

Begin: In the name of the Father (+) and of the Son and of the Holy Spirit. Amen.

Crucifix: Lord Jesus, when we are lost, how can we know the way? You are the way and the truth and the life, and no one comes to the Father except through you. Amen.

First bead, pray: Holy Mary, Mother of Christ our Lord, pray for us when we are lost; be our light in darkness, our help in times of trial. Amen.

Three beads, pray: Christ, you are the way, the truth, and the life. Lead us on the way; teach us your truth; bring us to everlasting life. Amen.

Second bead, pray: Holy Mary, Mother of Christ our Lord, pray for us when we are lost; be our light in darkness, our help in times of trial. Amen.

Announce first mystery for the day (see below):

Ten decade beads, pray: Holy Mary, Mother of God, bearer of the Word made flesh, pray for us when we are lost in sin; rejoice with us when we are found in Christ. Amen.

Conclude each decade with the Our Father.

Continue to the next mystery for the day.

MYSTERIES OF THE WAY (MONDAY, WEDNESDAY, FRIDAY)

Path of Life
"You show me the path of life.
In your presence there is fullness of joy;
in your right hand are pleasures for evermore."

PSALM 16:11

Holy Way
"A highway shall be there,
and it shall be called the Holy Way;
the unclean shall not travel on it,
but it shall be for God's people;
no traveller, not even fools, shall go astray."

ISAIAH 35:8

Way of Rest

Thus says the Lord:
Stand at the crossroads, and look,
and ask for the ancient paths,
where the good way lies; and walk in it,
and find rest for your souls....

JEREMIAH 6:16

Seeking the Door: "Ask, and it will be given to you; search, and you will find; knock, and the door will be opened for you" (Matthew 7:7).

The Narrow Gate: "Enter through the narrow gate; for the gate is wide and the road is easy that leads to destruction, and there are many who take it" (Matthew 7:13).

MYSTERIES OF THE TRUTH (TUESDAY AND SATURDAY)

Enduring Truth

Enter his gates with thanksgiving,
and his courts with praise.
Give thanks to him, bless his name.
For the Lord is good;
his steadfast love endures for ever,
and his faithfulness to all generations.

PSALM 100:4–5

Belonging to Truth: "They do not belong to the world, just as I do not belong to the world. Sanctify them in the truth; your word is truth" (John 17:16–17).

Rejoicing in Truth: "[Love] does not rejoice in wrongdoing, but rejoices in the truth" (1 Corinthians 13:6).

Thinking on Truth: "…whatever is true, whatever is honourable, whatever is just, whatever is pure, whatever is pleasing, whatever is commendable, if there is any excellence and if there is anything worthy of praise, think about these things" (Philippians 4:8).

Obeying Truth: "Now that you have purified your souls by your obedience to the truth so that you have genuine mutual love, love one another deeply from the heart" (1 Peter 1:22).

MYSTERIES OF THE LIFE (THURSDAY AND SUNDAY)

The Death of Death

And he will destroy on this mountain
*   the shroud that is cast over all peoples,*
*   the sheet that is spread over all nations;*
he will swallow up death for ever.
Then the Lord God will wipe away the tears from all faces…

ISAIAH 25:7–8

Exchanging One's Life: "For what will it profit them if they gain the whole world but forfeit their life? Or what will they give in return for their life?" (Matthew 16:26).

Losing One's Life: "Those who love their life lose it, and those who hate their life in this world will keep it for eternal life" (John 12:25).

Sacrificing One's Life: "For the Son of Man came not to be served but to serve, and to give his life a ransom for many" (Mark 10:45).

Eating from the Tree of Life: "Let anyone who has an ear listen to what the Spirit is saying to the churches. To everyone who conquers, I will give permission to eat from the tree of life that is in the paradise of God" (Revelation 2:7).

Concluding Prayer: Blessed Mary, Mother of all graces, Christ Jesus your son gave his life for the sins of the world so that all may live. At the foot of his cross, you wept with John his beloved disciple, mourning as only a mother could. Weep for us too when we wander from the narrow way, imperiling our eternal lives with sin. May we hear you crying for us and return to your motherly care. We long to rejoice with you at the throne of heaven! Pray for us that we may follow the way, know the truth, and live the life eternal. Amen.

Part Four
Prayers

Prayer for an Examination of Conscience

Opening Prayer

Lord of mercy, I delight in your love and desire nothing more than to come to you washed of all my sins, wholly righteous in your sight. Lead me to search my heart and mind, to remember all those times that I have failed to follow your way of gospel truth and perfecting love. You give your children the gifts of wisdom, understanding, counsel, fortitude, piety, knowledge, and awe of your majesty. Help me to search my conscience, to confess all my sins against these gifts, and to turn to you for your assurance of mercy and forgiveness. Amen.

Scripture Reading

A shoot shall come out from the stock of Jesse,
*   and a branch shall grow out of his roots.*
The spirit of the Lord shall rest on him,
*   the spirit of wisdom and understanding,*
*   the spirit of counsel and might,*
*   the spirit of knowledge and the fear of the Lord.*
His delight shall be in the fear of the Lord.

He shall not judge by what his eyes see,
*   or decide by what his ears hear;*
but with righteousness he shall judge the poor,
*   and decide with equity for the meek of the earth;*
he shall strike the earth with the rod of his mouth,
*   and with the breath of his lips he shall kill the wicked.*
Righteousness shall be the belt around his waist,
*   and faithfulness the belt around his loins.*

ISAIAH 11:2–5

The Examination

Lord, you have given me the gift of piety so that I might honor you as my Father. Bring to mind all those times that I failed to give you the worship you are due, all those times that my fervor for your Word has been lukewarm, all those times that my lack of fidelity to your law of love has led me away from you and your people. Strengthen my resolve to confess my sins against the duty to worship you with my whole heart, body, mind, and spirit.

Lord, you have given me the gift of knowledge so that I might know you to the limits of my ability as your creature. Bring to mind all those times that I have failed to seek out and find you in the beauty of your creation. All those times that I have allowed my intellectual gifts to be idled by distraction and deceit. All those times that I heave rejected the truth of your teachings and falsely judged the goodness of your creation in willful ignorance. Strengthen my resolve to confess my sins against the duty to see and hear your self-revelation in the pursuit of divine knowledge.

Lord, you have given me the gift of fortitude so that I might triumph over the temptations of this world. Bring to mind all those times that I have succumbed to spiritual cowardice by surrendering to compromise, deceit, and the opinions of men. All those times that I have allowed convenience, popularity, and fear of ridicule to ruin my courage. All those times that I have failed to encourage in others the virtue of a faithful heart in the pursuit of holiness. Strengthen my resolve to confess my sins against the duty to stand firm against temptation, falsehood, and oppression.

Lord, you have given me the gift of counsel so that I might always choose rightly when confronted with the temptation to follow my own way instead of yours. Bring to mind all those times that I have set aside this gift in order to prefer my will over yours; all those times that I have used false notions of the good, the true, and the beautiful to justify my selfish choices; all those times that I have failed to heed your voice of intuition and chose instead a path into darkness. Strengthen my resolve to confess my sins against the duty to listen to your small, still voice guiding me on the path to eternal life.

Lord, you have given me the gift of awe so that I might love you as children love their mother and father. Bring to mind all those times that I have not loved you as I ought. All those times that I have failed to honor you and my parents as you have commanded us to do. All those times that I have allowed a stubborn heart or closed mind to refuse obedience when obedience leads to your truth. Strengthen my resolve to confess my sins against the duty to show you filial love and respect and to treat my family and friends with honor.

Lord, you have given me the gift of understanding so that I might stand under the divine mysteries and contemplate the truths of heaven. Bring to mind all those times that I have attached my thoughts, words, and deeds to ignorance and malice. All those times that I have allowed my affections to lead me to vanity and pride. All those times that I have ignored the prompting of your Holy Spirit to see more clearly and more justly. Strengthen my resolve to confess my sins against the duty to apprehend your certain truths and live in righteousness.

Lord, you have given me the gift of wisdom so that I might rightly judge the impermanent things of this world against the permanence of your kingdom. Bring to mind all those times that I have failed to live my life as a means to my eternal end, all those times that I have used others for my selfish purposes, all those times that I have abused your gift of wisdom by failing to perfect my trust in you. Strengthen my resolve to confess my sins against the duty to know and understand my life as a gift with an eternal goal and the lives of others as your revelation of divine love.

Holy Spirit, giver of life eternal, with the Father and the Son, my one true God, I praise you and give you thanks for your gifts. I give myself to you and unite myself to the rightful worship you receive from all the angels, saints, and the pilgrim Church.

O Giver of all gifts, you filled the soul of the Blessed Mother of God with abundant grace. Sinless, she came into this world and left it to join you in heaven. I ask you to shine your divine light on my faults and show me the many ways I have failed to do my baptismal duty to you and your Church. With your help I am sure to confess all my sins, receive your forgiveness, and do the good work you have given me to do. Though I despair for my sins, I never doubt your love and mercy. In Christ's name, I pray. Amen.

The ABC Prayer for Conversion

O Lord, to come to you is to turn from sin. In answer to the persistent urging of your Holy Spirit, I come to you, confessing my sins and asking your forgiveness. Turn me, O Lord, away from my offenses and renew in me a clean heart.

Turn me, O Lord, away from…
>   Acquisitiveness, anxiety, apostasy, and avarice;
>   Blasphemy, belittlements, berating, brooding;
>   Calumny, covetousness, cruelty, and cursing.

Turn me, O Lord, away from…
>   Death, debt, despair, and distraction;
>   Egoism, envy, error, and evil;
>   Falsity, fatalism, fear, and fraud.

Turn me, O Lord, away from…
>   Glamour, gluttony, grandiosity, and greed;
>   Hatred, heckling, hopelessness, and hurt;
>   Indecency, ignorance, infidelity, and injustice.

Turn me, O Lord, away from…
>   Jealousy, jeering, jocularity, and judgment;
>   Lawlessness, libel, lust, and lying;
>   Materialism, meddling, mocking, and murder.

Turn me, O Lord, away from…
>   Nagging, narcissism, negligence, and nihilism;
>   Obstinacy, occultism, omission, ostentatious display;
>   Pessimism, presumption, pride, and privilege.

Turn me, O Lord, away from…
>   Qualms in faith, quarrelling, quick-temperedness, quietism,
>   Rage, rancor, rashness, and relativism;
>   Sadness, sarcasm, subversion, and sullenness.

Turn me, O Lord, away from...
　　Temptation, tawdriness, timidity, treachery;
　　Uncleanliness, unctuousness, usury, usurpation;
　　Vainglory, vengeance, violence, and vexation.
Turn me, O Lord, to you in zealous faith. Amen.

Prayer Before Reconciliation

Weakened by my sins, strengthened by your mercy, I come to you, Lord, confessing my failures to love you and my neighbors as I ought.

Restore us again, O God of our salvation,
* and put away your indignation towards us.*
Will you be angry with us for ever?
* Will you prolong your anger to all generations?*
Will you not revive us again,
* so that your people may rejoice in you?*
Show us your steadfast love, O Lord,
* and grant us your salvation.*

PSALM 85:4–7

Subdue my pride, shackle my vanity, free my tongue, and I will let go of every fault, every failure, every sin. Lift up my praise, unchain my love, free my heart, and I will welcome your mercy as light for my darkness. Amen.

Prayer After Reconciliation

Lord, let my prayer of thanksgiving rise to you! Freed from my sins and cleansed from my guilt, I devote myself again to the work of growing holy in your love.

Praise the Lord!
Praise the Lord!
Praise, O servants of the Lord;
*   praise the name of the Lord.*

Blessed be the name of the Lord
*   from this time on and for evermore.*
From the rising of the sun to its setting
*   the name of the Lord is to be praised.*
The Lord is high above all nations,
*   and his glory above the heavens.*

PSALM 113:1–4

You have no need of my praise! Yet I cannot but give you praise for your mercy. Thank you, Lord, for the gift of your Son. Be with me and those I love as I continue on the Way to you. Amen.

For a Dark Night of the Soul

Opening Prayer

Lord of Light, a dark night has fallen on my soul. Though the star of your wisdom never sets, I cannot see it, and I expect no dawn. Weighted down with the burdens of this life, I am weakened in suffering and plagued by doubt. Faith is a sieve, hope a chain. Love is lost and will not be found. All I do seems futile. My cross is too heavy, and my way is littered with sharp stones. Another step without you, and I will fall. I come to you in mourning, grieving the loss of your light. I have seen and want to see again. I have heard and want to hear again. Is wanting enough? Is my longing for you strong enough to see me through?

Scripture Reading

"Why is light given to one who cannot see the way,
*   whom God has fenced in?*
For my sighing comes like my bread,
*   and my groanings are poured out like water.*
Truly the thing that I fear comes upon me,
*   and what I dread befalls me.*
I am not at ease, nor am I quiet;
*   I have no rest; but trouble comes."*
O that I might have my request,
*   and that God would grant my desire;*
that it would please God to crush me,
*   that he would let loose his hand and cut me off!*
This would be my consolation;
*   I would even exult in unrelenting pain;*
*   for I have not denied the words of the Holy One.*

What is my strength, that I should wait?
   And what is my end, that I should be patient?
Is my strength the strength of stones,
   or is my flesh bronze?
In truth I have no help in me,
   and any resource is driven from me.

JOB 3:23–26; 6:8–13

Closing Prayer

Lord, show me the limits of this darkness. Move the shadows with your light. Bring dawn to my suffering. If I have abandoned your Word, speak it to me once more. If I have rejected your wisdom, make me wise in your ways. If I have failed to see your work in my life, open my eyes so that I might know your will. I do not ask that you lift my burdens, only that I may know you are with me in the darkness. You are my strength and my consolation, my purpose and my path. I am lost. Be with me in this dark night, and I will rejoice at sunrise! In Christ's holy name. Amen.

Daily Morning Prayer

Begin: Lord, free my tongue, (+) and I will praise your name all the day long! Gloria.

Daily Hymn

O sing to the Lord a new song;
  sing to the Lord, all the earth.
Sing to the Lord, bless his name;
  tell of his salvation from day to day.
Declare his glory among the nations,
  his marvellous works among all the peoples.
For great is the Lord, and greatly to be praised;
  he is to be revered above all gods.
For all the gods of the peoples are idols,
  but the Lord made the heavens.
Honour and majesty are before him;
  strength and beauty are in his sanctuary.

PSALM 96:1–6

Daily Psalms

Antiphon: A new dawn rises on his creation; His Word brings light from night's darkness. (Recite antiphon before the psalm.)

Sunday for exultation of the Lord: Psalm 148, 150
Monday for strength in faith: Psalm 5
Tuesday for joyful thanksgiving: Psalm 33:1–12
Wednesday for integrity: Psalm 26
Thursday for victory in the Lord: Psalm 113:1–14
Friday for repentance: Psalm 51
Saturday for refuge in the Lord: Psalm 11

(Repeat the antiphon after the psalm and say the Gloria.)

Scripture Reading: Choose one of the lesser known letters from the New Testament (Titus; Philemon; 1 and 2 Peter; 1, 2, and 3 John; or Jude) and read a small portion each morning.

Consecrate the Day: Lord, today I put away falsehood. Let me speak only the truth to my friends and neighbors. Let no evil word come from my mouth. I will praise your name to all I meet. Today, with your grace, I put away greed and laziness. I will labor honestly with my own hands and share with the least among your children. I put away wrath and vengeance. There is no room in my life for the spirits of hatred and bitterness. The sun will not set on my anger. Today, with your grace, I put away all backbiting and slander, all malice and insult. I will not offend your Holy Spirit! I am marked with his seal for the day of my redemption, and my heart will not turn from you. With the help of your grace, I set aside this day to be kind, open-hearted, forgiving, zealous in faith, steadfast in witness, and always humble before my faults. As I am forgiven, so I forgive. As I am loved, so I love. Lord, today and always, I am yours. Do with me as you will. Amen.

Closing Prayer: Our Father...

Daily Evening Prayer

Begin: Lord, be with me as night falls, (+) and I will rest in your Spirit always! Gloria.

Daily Hymn

Out of the depths I cry to you, O Lord.
Lord, hear my voice!
Let your ears be attentive
to the voice of my supplications!

If you, O Lord, should mark iniquities,
Lord, who could stand?
But there is forgiveness with you,
so that you may be revered.

I wait for the Lord, my soul waits,
and in his word I hope;
my soul waits for the Lord
more than those who watch for the morning,
more than those who watch for the morning.

PSALM 130:1–6

Daily Psalms

Antiphon: As night falls on his creation, the Word shines brighter for his people! (Recite antiphon before the psalm.)

Sunday for praising God: Psalm 148, 150
Monday for the Lord's power: Psalm 90
Tuesday for mercy: Psalm 57
Wednesday for deliverance: Psalm 3
Thursday for a just cause: Psalm 17

Friday for salvation from enemies: Psalm 18:1–15
Saturday for calling on the Lord: Psalm 141

(Repeat the antiphon after the psalm and say the Gloria.)

Scripture Reading: Continue reading a small portion from the Scripture you chose this morning.

Examination of Your Consecrated Day

Lord, today I tried to put away falsehood. Did I speak only the truth to my friends and neighbors? Did any evil word come out from my mouth? Did I praise your name to all I met? Today, with your grace, I worked to put away greed and laziness. Did I labor honestly with my own hands and share with the least among your children? Did I put away wrath and vengeance? Where have I left room in my life for the spirits of hatred and bitterness? The sun will not set on my anger! Today, with your grace, I worked to put away all backbiting and slander, all malice and insult. Did I offend your Holy Spirit? My heart will not turn from you. With the help of your grace, I set out this morning to be kind, open-hearted, forgiving, zealous in faith, steadfast in witness, and always humble before my faults. Did I succeed? Where I did not, forgive my failures, Lord. Bring me closer to your perfection. This night and always, I am yours. Do with me as you will. Amen.

Closing Prayer: Our Father...

Sources and Permissions

Cyprian of Carthage, "On the Lord's Prayer." Translated by Rev. Ernest Wallis, Ph.D. in *The Early Church Fathers and Other Works*, Wm. B. Eerdmans Pub. Co., Edinburgh, Scotland: 1867.

Excerpts from *Gregory of Nyssa: The Life of Moses*, translation, introduction and notes by Everett Ferguson and Abraham J. Malherbe. Copyright © 1978 by Paulist Press, Paulist Press, Inc., New York/Mahwah, NJ. Reprinted by permission of Paulist Press, Inc. www.paulistpress.com.

Excerpts from *Meister Eckhart: The Essential Sermons, Commentaries, Treatises, and Defense*, translated and introduced by Edmund Colledge, O.S.A. and Bernard McGinn, Copyright © 1981 by Paulist Press, Paulist Press, Inc., New York/Mahwah, NJ. Reprinted by permission of Paulist Press, Inc. www.paulistpress.com.

Murray, Father Paul Murray, OP. "Recovering the Contemplative Dimension." Presented to the General Chapter of the Dominican Order. Providence, RI: July 2001.

Pope Benedict XVI. *Deus Caritas Est*, Encyclical Letter of the Supreme Pontiff to the Bishops, Priests, and Deacons, Men and Women, Religious and All the Lay Faithful on Christian Love: 2005.

———. *Spe Salvi*, Encyclical Letter of the Supreme Pontiff to the Bishops Priests and Deacons Men and Women Religious and All the Lay Faithful on Christian Hope: 2007.

Radcliffe, Father Timothy, OP. "'A city set on a hilltop cannot be hidden': A Contemplate Life." Presented at Santa Sabina, Rome on the Feast of St. Catherine of Siena, 2001.

———. "The Wellspring of Hope: Study and the Annunciation of the Good News." Presented at Santa Sabina, Rome: October 1996.

———. "Vowed to Mission" (Letter to the Order). Santa Sabina, Rome: 1994.

St. Augustine. "Sermon to Catechumins on the Creed." Translated by H. Browne in *Nicene and Post-Nicene Fathers*, First Series, Vol. 3. Edited by Philip Schaff. Christian Literature Publishing Co., Buffalo, NY: 1887. Revised and edited for New Advent by Kevin Knight. Adapted for this publication by the author.

St. Basil the Great, "Treatise on the Holy Spirit" (*De Spiritu Sancto*). Translated by Blomfield Jackson in *Nicene and Post-Nicene Fathers*, Second Series, Vol. 8. Edited by Philip Schaff and Henry Wace. Christian Literature Publishing Co., Buffalo, NY: 1895. Revised and edited for New Advent by Kevin Knight.